THE POLYNESIAN ICONOCLASM

ASAO Studies in Pacific Anthropology

General Editor: Rupert Stasch, Department of Anthropology,
University of California, San Diego

The Association for Social Anthropology in Oceania (ASAO) is an international organization dedicated to studies of Pacific cultures, societies, and histories. This series publishes monographs and thematic collections on topics of global and comparative significance, grounded in anthropological fieldwork in Pacific locations.

The Polynesian Iconoclasm
Religious Revolution and the Seasonality of Power

Jeffrey Sissons

berghahn
NEW YORK · OXFORD
www.berghahnbooks.com

First published in 2014 by

Berghahn Books

www.berghahnbooks.com

©2014 Jeffrey Sissons

Library of Congress Cataloging-in-Publication Data

Sissons, Jeffrey.
  The Polynesian iconoclasm : religious revolution and the seasonality of power / Jeffrey
Sissons. — First edition.
        pages cm
  Includes bibliographical references.
  ISBN 978-1-78238-413-7 (hardback : alk. paper) — ISBN 978-1-78238-414-4 (ebook)
  1. Polynesia—Church history. I. Title.
  BR1495.P6S57 2014
  996—dc23

                                                                      2014000901

British Library Cataloguing in Publication Data

A catalogue record for this book is available from the British Library

Printed on acid-free paper.

ISBN: 978-1-78238-413-7 hardback
ISBN: 978-1-78238-414-4 ebook

Contents

Figures

Acknowledgements 🐾

My interest in the events described in this book began more than twenty-five years ago when I visited Rarotonga and Mangaia in the Southern Cook Islands intending to study traditional history. I remain very grateful to Teaea Parima and his family for welcoming me into their home at Tamarua and introducing me to daily life on Mangaia. Although I soon abandoned my historical project, the one article that resulted from it, 'The Seasonality of Power: The Rarotongan Legend of Tangiia' (Sissons 1989), became the seed for the present work.

Returning to Rarotonga in 1992, I embarked upon a new study of culture and nationhood in the Cook Islands (Sissons 1999). Understanding the processes of nation-building in the Cook Islands required me to make sense of the contrasting relationship between the sacred ruins of pre-Christian temples (*marae*) and the much more highly visible Christian churches – the former indexing continuities of local power and the latter indexing Christian nationhood. I was extremely fortunate at this time to be able to draw upon the wise guidance of Ron Crocombe, Kauraka Kauraka, Sir Tom Davis, Jon Jonassen, George Paniani, Rod Dixon, Makiuti and Polly Tongia and Richard Walter, to all of whom I remain extremely grateful.

In 2001 while on a visiting fellowship at Goldsmith's College, University of London, I became interested in the fate and identities of Cook Islands god-images that had been sent to the heart of empire by London Missionary Society missionaries and which were then being moved from the Museum of Mankind to the British Museum. I visited the London Missionary Society archives, housed at the School of Oriental and African Studies, in search of more information about these images and quickly discovered that they were the victims of a much larger destructive event. I am particularly grateful to Nicholas Thomas for facilitating the Goldsmith's fellowship and for his subsequent encouragement and support for this project.

The research for and writing of this book during the period 2009–2012 was generously supported by a grant from the Marsden Fund. In addition to providing relief from teaching duties, this grant enabled me to spend an additional six weeks in the London archives and to spend time in the Society Islands visiting a number of key sites discussed in this book. In this regard, I am particularly grateful to Ato Frogier for showing me the site of the first Polynesian printing press, established on Moʻorea in 1817, and for helping me understand the destruction of *marae* there.

Initial attempts to make sense of events associated with the Polynesian Iconoclasm resulted in four articles, written while this larger work was in preparation (Sissons 2007, 2008, 2011a, 2011b). In all cases, the arguments made in these articles differ significantly from those made here. Versions of the articles were presented as seminars in the School of Social and Cultural Sciences at Victoria University, and I thank my colleagues, particularly James Urry, for their engagement with the ideas. I also take this opportunity to warmly thank Alan Strathern, Rupert Stasch and an anonymous reviewer for their helpful comments on an initial version of the manuscript.

The images from early-nineteenth-century books held by Victoria University of Wellington Library were photographed by ITS Image Services. I am grateful to Robert Cross for his fine work and to the staff of the J. C. Beaglehole Room for their assistance in locating the original images.

Finally, I would like to thank my son, Hugo, for the many excellent photographs he took in the Society Islands, several of which are included here, and my wife, Catherine, for her loving support and stimulating theological engagement with my project.

Abbreviations

LMS   London Missionary Society

QC   *Quarterly Chronicle*, undated publication of the London Missionary Society, World Council of Missions collection

SSJ   South Seas Journals, London Missionary Society Collection, School of Oriental and African Studies

SSL   South Seas Letters, London Missionary Society Collection, School of Oriental and African Studies

Map of Polynesia and Other Pacific Islands 🍀

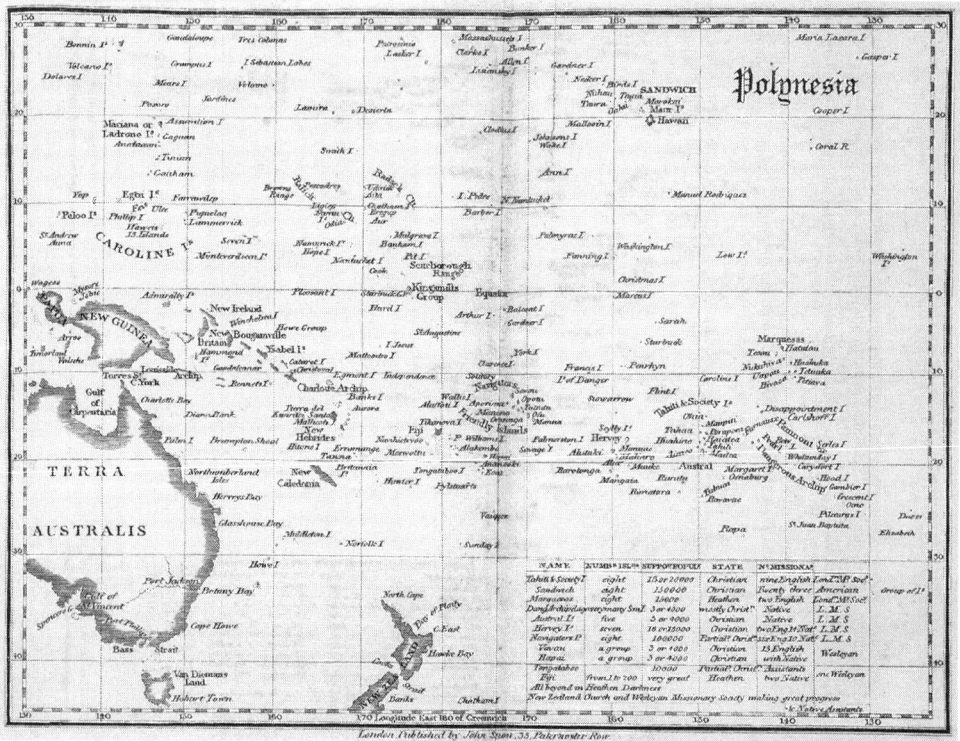

Source: Williams (1838). Victoria University of Wellington.

Introduction 🏵
Exploding History

The Polynesian Iconoclasm was an explosive event of world-historical significance. It began on the island of Mo'orea, Tahiti's close neighbour, in the winter of 1815 when district priests and chiefs demonstrated their allegiance to a high chief, Pomare, and his new god, Jehova, by destroying their sacrificial altars and god-images. The following summer, district chiefs in Tahiti and most other Society Islands did likewise, desecrating all of their images and temples. Within ten years, Society Islanders would take their iconoclastic revolution to the Austral Islands, Hawai'i and the Southern Cook Islands. In each place iconoclastic performances, probably none of which were witnessed by European missionaries, would be staged. This was the Polynesian Iconoclasm, an event of anthropological moment, not simply because of the radical social changes that it initiated but, equally importantly, because of the *manner* in which things changed.

Marshall Sahlins has famously argued that Captain Cook's arrival in Hawai'i in 1778–1779 was, for Hawaiians, a seasonal event of ritual significance, his arrival coinciding with the annual return of the fertility god, Lono. I will argue here that the Polynesian Iconoclasm, an event that occurred some forty years later and on a much larger scale than Cook's arrival, was of related seasonal and ritual significance for Polynesians. Like Cook's arrival, almost all destructive episodes of the Polynesian Iconoclasm occurred during the November to January period. Termed *makahiki* in Hawai'i and *matari'i-i-nia* in Tahiti, this was the season when gods and ancestors returned to bring about a renewal of life. If Cook was treated as such a god, Jehova was to be the real thing.

Tahiti and all of the societies that participated in Pomare's revolution were characterized by a seasonality of power in that they all had pre-existing traditions of seasonal social renewal during which the political order was annually dissolved and reconstituted. Hawai'i's *makahiki* and the subsequent *luakini* temple rites though which hierarchy was re-asserted are the most anthropologically well-known of these via the work of Sahlins (1985) and Valeri (1985). Others included contrasting *parara'a matahiti* and *pa'iatua* rites in the Society Islands and contrasting *pure ari'i* and *takurua* rites in the Southern Cook Islands. All of these contrasting rites of hierarchical dissolution and social reconstitution were seasonal events, the two forms of rite occurring some six months apart.

Prior to the iconoclasms, rites of hierarchy entailed building, re-building or re-consecrating temples; after the iconoclasms this seasonal labour was channelled, instead, into the building of Christian temples. The rapid spread of Pomare's iconoclastic revolution was partly due to the centralizing nature of the regionally-shared rites of seasonal renewal. The social transformations that followed the destruction were, in all cases, towards even greater centralization, resulting in the creation of societies that, like Britain, had Jehova as their ultimate source of *mana*. In time, new forms of power would be creatively improvised, neither entirely 'sovereign' nor entirely 'disciplinary' (in Foucault's senses of these terms). Significantly, in the Marquesas Islands and New Zealand, east Polynesian neighbours whose seasonal rituals were more localized and less centralizing than those in the societies considered here, large-scale conversions to Christianity did not occur until the 1850s.

As Marshall Sahlins saw it in 1985, the problem was to 'explode the concept of history by the anthropological experience of culture'. He continued:

> The heretofore obscure histories of remote islands deserve a place alongside the self-contemplation of the European past – or the history of "civilizations" – for their own remarkable contributions to historical understanding. We can multiply our conceptions of history by the diversity of structures. Suddenly, there are all kinds of new things to consider. (Sahlins 1985: 72)

I agree with Sahlins that there is a need to better understand the diversity of structures that have guided different modes of historical practice and this book is an anthropological contribution to such an endeavour.

The iconoclastic priests of Moʻorea were, like the many priests across eastern Polynesia who later improvised upon their performances, engaging in a particular mode of historical practice that Sahlins has termed 'mythopraxis' but that I shall term 'rituopraxis'. For Sahlins, mythopraxis was a Polynesian mode of chiefly historical action in which enduring cultural schemas, precoded in myth and tradition, were put into practice. A dramatic example of such action for Sahlins was the cutting down of a British flagpole by the New Zealand Maori chief, Hone Heke. By cutting down this flag-pole four times between July 1844 and March 1845, Heke was, according to Sahlins, sending a message to other chiefs that this was a British shrine (*tuahu*) that symbolized British claims to sovereignty. Heke's actions were mythopraxis because he and his allies recognized a double equivalence: firstly, between the British flagpole and the ritual poles of their shrines and secondly, between these poles and those used by the mythical ancestor, Tane, to prop up the sky-father after he had been separated from the earth-mother. The British had put in place the equivalent of one of Tane's poles in order to create a life-enhancing space for themselves.

In contrast to Sahlins, I prioritize the structure of practice over the structure of myth. While Sahlins derived cultural schemas from pre-existing myth and tradition, I derive them from pre-existing ritual practice. I do recognize a duality of structure in that the meaning of ritual practice is often encoded in myths and traditions. Still, taking my inspiration from the practice theory of Pierre Bourdieu, I accord primacy to the temporal, embodied structures of ritual life (Sissons 1989: 354).

Indeed, I think Heke's iconoclastic actions towards the British flagpole might best be conceptualized as rituopraxis – as improvisations upon ritual precedents. Rather than liken the British flagpole to the relatively small 'staves' or 'wands' erected by priests at their shrines (Best 1972: 1072–73), Heke and his allies were equally likely to have regarded the British flagpole as a *pou rahui* (also termed *pou whenua*), a pole erected by chiefs to assert claims over land and resources. Sahlins himself recognized this to be an alternative interpretation (1985: 63n32). *Pou rahui* were large poles, sometimes decorated with carved representations of human faces, set up to mark boundaries or signify that an area was *tapu* and thus under sacred protection. Conflicts over chiefly *mana* and rights to land often centred on such poles, and a pole erected by one chief was sometimes torn or burned down by the supporters of an opposing chief (Best 2005 [1924] II: 185–89). If Heke understood the British flagpole to have been an assertion by a British Governor of his *mana* (authority) over Heke's tribal lands then the chief's praxis did not so much enact the precedent of mythical narrative as the precedent of ritual conflict. His rituopraxis was an improvisation upon a temporal logic of challenge and riposte centred on poles and having as its motor a sense of *mana,* a chiefly disposition or *habitus.*

Sahlins was himself one of the first anthropologists to recognize the value of Bourdieu's notions of *habitus* and improvisation for understanding historical change. Although he has been described as a historical practice theorist (Ortner 1984: 155–56; 1989: 11), the profound influence of Bourdieu on Sahlins's thought has often been under-estimated. *Habitus,* for Sahlins, comprised the 'unreflected premises' of historical action in a 'performative' mode, a mode of action distinct from mythopraxis (1985: 29). For Hawaiian commoners who had, by the late eighteenth and early nineteenth centuries, surrendered the prescriptive genealogical and mythical dimension of social life to ruling chiefs, culture was mostly 'lived' 'in practice and as *habitus*', their lives,

> run on an unconscious mastery of the system … together with the homespun concepts of the good that allow[ed] them to improvise daily activities on the level of the pragmatic and matter-of-fact. Such unreflective mastery of percept and precept is what Bourdieu calls *habitus.* (1985: 51)

I differ from Sahlins, however, in extending the explanatory concept of *habitus* from the lives of commoners to include the political lives of chiefs and priests. The Polynesian chiefs and priests that we will meet in this book, although having different hierarchically conditioned dispositions from common people (including a greater interest in things cosmological), participated with them in rituopraxis, seasonally orchestrating conversion processes and taking leading roles in ritual improvisation. This orchestration was performative historical action loosely structured by *habitus*.

In the programmatic opening sentences of *Islands of History,* the book in which he argued the need for an explosion of history, Sahlins wrote:

> History is culturally ordered, differently so in different societies, according to meaningful schemes of things. The converse is also true: cultural schemes are historically ordered, since to a greater or lesser extent the meanings are revalued as they are practically enacted. The synthesis of these contraries unfolds in the creative action of historic subjects, the people concerned. (Sahlins 1985: vii)

In my view, this applies equally well to the relationship between history and *habitus*. History is also ordered according to practical schemas and embodied *habitus,* differently so in different societies. And the converse is also true: practical schemas and *habitus* are transformed within history.

In Sahlins's and Kirch's superb historical ethnography, *Anahulu, Volume One,* this more Bourdieusian view of structure is, at times, also clearly evident. Writing of the *makahiki* rites during which hierarchy was partly suspended (and he might also have included the subsequent *Luakini* rites during which hierarchy was re-imposed), Sahlins concluded:

> Clearly the Makahiki is a structure of the long run, an enduring organizing principle of Hawaiian history. The expression of a total cultural order projected on the calendrical plane, it continued to inhabit the rhythms and content of Hawaiian social life long after 1819 when the old gods had been consigned to the flames. There it was: a recurrent cycle of meaning and affect, popular as well as priestly, that could be drawn on to represent forces of the conjuncture never dreamed of in the ancient philosophy. (1992: 121)

This book will show that a seasonal schema of ritual totalization also continued to structure transformations throughout much of eastern Polynesia in the aftermath of other, regionally connected, iconoclasms. But in addition to this, it argues that the timing of the iconoclastic episodes themselves, as improvised acts of rituopraxis, conformed to such a seasonal logic. Sahlins deliberately de-emphasized the dramatic significance of the Hawaiian iconoclasm, in part, no doubt, because he sought to reveal cultural continuities in Hawaiian history and also, perhaps, because this event had already been closely analysed by more than a few anthropologists and historians. But in treating the iconoclasm in this way, its significance as an improvised rite of totalizing regeneration, intimately connected to others that occurred in eastern Polynesia during the same period, was left under-appreciated.

Today, following Sahlins's earlier call to explode the concept of history, we are also required to oppose a now influential particular concept of history, Nietzschean genealogy, which Foucault characterized as 'effective' history (Foucault 1984a: 59). This concept of history rejects all 'immobile forms that precede the external world of accident and succession.' In this conception, subjects are products of, but never producers of, history. The practice history I attempt here is pitched against this alternative form of history which seeks to 'dispense with the constituent subject, to get rid of the subject itself' (ibid.).

The originality and appeal of Foucault's historical works are due largely to their genealogical character. Summarizing his genealogical project in an interview with Paul Rabinow and Herbert Dreyfus, Foucault explained that three domains of genealogy were possible: A historical ontology or 'effective history' of ourselves firstly, 'in relation to truth through which we constitute ourselves as subjects of knowledge', secondly 'in relation to a field of power through which we constitute ourselves as subjects acting on others', and thirdly 'in relation to ethics through which we constitute ourselves as moral subjects' (Foucault 1984b: 351). Thus, for Foucault, genealogy was ultimately about self-constituting subjects. Indeed, as Sahlins has correctly pointed out, Foucault dissolved cultural forms into subjugation effects so that in the end 'the only thing left standing is the subject' (Sahlins 2004: 248). Sahlins scathingly described this approach as 'subjectology' (Sahlins 2002: 68).

Conveniently hidden in Foucault's phrase 'we constitute ourselves as subjects' is the fact that the 'we' doing the constituting must already be subjects – we are never pre-subjects. The question then, one which Foucault was unable to ask, let alone answer, is what is the relationship between the constituting and constituted subject? Bourdieu provides one answer: It is a relationship mediated through practical schemas and *habitus*. Practice history is therefore directly opposed to genealogy in that it is concerned with the ways that we *re*-constitute ourselves as subjects through strategic improvisations that imply continuities of *habitus* (see Bourdieu 2008: 191n3, where Bourdieu distances himself from Foucault).

While I seek to develop here a practice-theory approach to history that draws generally on Bourdieu's work, I have not found all of the devices in his conceptual tool-kit to be equally helpful in understanding the events described. In particular, his notion of the 'field' as a hyper-competitive arena in which people occupying different positions struggle over the definition and possession of 'symbolic capital' does not, for me, represent any significant conceptual advance over the old-fashioned notion of a hierarchically organized 'society'. It is perhaps no accident that his economistic representation of social life as animated by competition for capital has found such wide favour among competitive, strongly individualistic, university scholars. In fact, Bourdieu's representation of social life as a competitive game merely elevates one type of social practice to the status of a model for all others. If we were going to have such a synecdocheal model, then a child's birthday party would serve equally well, probably better. Children's birthday parties are improvised occasions that are somehow alike yet always different from each other. They change with age, usually without following any explicit formula, following, instead, a 'fuzzy logic' that expresses both individualism and familialism. I am sure there are many other, equally arbitrary, models that could be used. I am dealing, in this book, with whole societies undergoing radical transformation. Although competitive struggles over the definition and distribution of symbolic capital were undoubtedly historically significant across the region, so too were practices and occasions expressing alliance and allegiance.

Bourdieu made it clear that understanding ritual practice 'means more than reconstituting its internal logic. It also means restoring its practical necessity by relating it to the real conditions of its genesis' (1980: 97). However, he also insisted that we need to do more than this. Ritual practice needs to be related to the material conditions of its genesis as these are apprehended via attitudes, orientations, 'urgencies' and schemes of perception embodied as *habitus. Habitus* includes a pre-reflective ethical sense – a practical sense of right and wrong, of appropriate and inappropriate engagement with material circumstances that vary with social position. *Habitus* becomes history when these various modes engage with each other in changing material circumstances (Bourdieu 2000: 148). Bourdieu did not, however, theorize radical social change in any sustained sense as I seek to do here, his interests being more focussed on the emergence and transformation of fields than on the nature of historical agency, radical or otherwise.

What I am terming 'rituopraxis' was a revolutionary mode of historical agency which, in eastern and central Polynesia, was orchestrated by both chiefs and priests. In the 1980s, Sahlins suggested the term 'heroic history' for the particular mode of historical change that ensued from chiefly agency in Polynesia. It was characterized by 'the sense of history as incorporated in the chiefly person and expressed in his current action.... Embodying and making history, ruling chiefs thus practice socially the capacities they are given cosmologically' (Sahlins 2000: 324–25). The main chiefly modes of 'making history' in Polynesia were undoubtedly war and ritual, and war itself was in many ways a part of the domain of ritual more generally (Sahlins 1985: 43–44). Hocart's description of the Fijian king is equally true for high chiefs of eastern Polynesia: 'his whole life is one course of ritual' (Hocart 1933: 245; Sahlins

2004: 161). But it is significant for the argument proposed in this book that war and ritual were also orchestrated by priests and involved, in different ways at different times, most of the population. Indeed, in many contexts, Sahlins's 'heroic history' might more usefully have been termed 'priestly history'. Priests in eastern Polynesia assumed leading roles in rituopraxis – they were social to-talizers in their actions and discourses. Having 'godly' dispositions, they were predisposed to interpret their social world cosmologically as they practically positioned themselves between gods and people and they were adept at devis-ing creative strategies for dealing with this relationship. They were experts at the timing and staging of ritual events – at knowing when, where and what to sacrifice.

The ritual praxis of priests and chiefs was, to use Sahlins's more recent term, largely 'systemic', in contrast to that of prophets – leaders made of the moment – whose agency was more 'conjunctural' (Sahlins 2004: 155–59). Priestly and chiefly orchestration also coincided, however, with what Bourdieu termed a 'conductorless orchestration which gives regularity, unity and syste-maticity to practices even in the absence of any spontaneous or imposed or-ganisation of individual projects' (1980: 59). In the Polynesian societies of this book, this 'conductorless orchestration' was performed to a seasonal rhythm. Commoner participation in the ritual remaking of their societies was, in some circumstances, forced or strongly directed, but it was also the expression of collective modes of hierarchically-conditioned *habitus* grounded in practices and experiences of seasonality. Commoners in heroic polities tended to at-tribute their own agency to the chief who, it was assumed, embodied the life of the whole society (Sahlins 1985: 35–54). However, as Bourdieu has noted, revolutionary transformations such as those discussed in this book could not have succeeded

> without a minimum of concordance between the *habitus* of the mobi-lizing agents (prophet, leader etc.) and the dispositions of those who recognized themselves in their practices and words, and, above all, without the inclination towards grouping that springs from the spon-taneous orchestration of dispositions. (Bourdieu 1980: 59)

Sahlins has again expressed a similar view. In accounting for popular re-bellions in Hawai'i in the late 1820s and 1830s, for example, he emphasized the importance of *habitus* and enduring logics of practice – in this case, a collec-tive spontaneity and seasonality formerly associated with the 'carnivalesque' *makahiki* – as mobilizing or orchestrating influences (Sahlins 1992: 122).

This book, then, is both a practice history and an anthropological med-itation on a particular form of historical agency. As I have already stressed, the societies that are the subject of this book – the Society Islands, Austral Islands, Southern Cook Islands and Hawaiian Islands – shared closely related traditions of seasonal regeneration. The first chapter describes and compares pre-Christian practices of seasonal renewal and their cosmological contexts across these several societies, as a foundation for the chapters which follow. The overall argument pursued in subsequent chapters is that the iconoclastic performances and subsequent forms of ritual centralisation were improvisations that brought into play practical logics and modes of hierarchically-conditioned *habitus* previously enacted in the seasonal traditions. It is not just that the timing of the iconoclastic events and subsequent reconstructions reproduced an earlier seasonality. Additionally, the existence of regionally-shared seasonal traditions of collective social renewal was crucial to the rapid spread of Pomare's revolution. It was the socially totalizing and centralizing qualities of seasonal rites founded on a cyclical temporality and collective participation that were of critical importance to the unfolding of the Polynesian Iconoclasm as a region-wide historical transformation.

More specifically, Chapter 2 focuses on the initial iconoclastic episodes on the island of Mo'orea and seeks to understand them as improvised reversals of rites of hierarchy, performed at the time when the chiefly order was normally reinstated. In Chapters 3 and 4 I consider the extension of this Mo'orean iconoclasm to the Society Islands, Austral Islands, Hawai'i and the Southern Cook Islands during the *makahiki* period or its equivalents. Analyzing these events, I engage with anthropological theories that address relationships between sacrifice and historical transformation and seek to build on Hocart's insights into the ritual dimensions of centralization. Chapter 5 considers the seasonal re-building of temples in the form of churches and (in Hawai'i) royal houses. These construction projects of architectural centralization entailed the mobilisation of mass labour from populations who traditionally signalled their allegiance to chiefs through the construction of their houses and temples. In Chapter 6 I reflect upon an association between the renewal of society through the re-construction of god-images and the production of Christian books, an association that has implications for anthropological theories of fetishism. In Chapter 7 I return to the seasonality of power, focussing on the imposition of new Christian tabus to replace former priestly-imposed sanctions, as well as resistance to these new tabus in the form of a return to seasonal *communitas*. I show that the public introduction of printed laws was a rite that loosely conformed to pre-Christian ritual cycles, and I go on to discuss episodes of 'judging' during which pre-Christian forms of symbolic domination and modes of *habitus* were put into play. The final chapter draws upon the preceding analyses to consider, more generally, relationships between history, *habitus* and seasonality and to reflect on the undeveloped significance of Bourdieu's practice theory for an understanding of historical change.

🕸 1

The Seasonality of Life

'Ritual, as long as it retains its meaning, is a co-operation for life.'
—Hocart, *Kings and Councillors*

While the timing of Captain Cook's arrival in Hawai'i during the *makahiki* season of 1778–1779 was a mere coincidence, the Polynesian Iconoclasm which occurred during the same or equivalent season across numerous different societies several decades later was anything but a chance occurrence. This timing was, instead, the outcome of collective agency deeply informed by local understandings and practices of seasonality. In the Society Islands, Hawai'i, the Austral Islands and the Southern Cook Islands, the mass destruction of temples and the destruction, concealment and defilement of god-images between the years 1815 and 1828 were ritual events, almost all initiated during the November to January period. In contrast, the subsequent openings of new temples in the form of large, chiefly chapels occurred, in most instances, during the months of May and June (see Appendix). In this chapter I lay the groundwork for the main arguments developed across this book by describing the ritualized seasonality of political and social life in eastern Polynesia and Hawai'i prior to Christian conversion. In subsequent chapters I seek to show how this seasonality provided meaning and structure to the processes of Christian conversion and the local rebellions that they provoked. Ritually produced seasonal cycles constituted a lived and embodied temporality for priests, chiefs and commoners alike; in other words, pre-Christian seasonality was embodied as differentiated, collective *habitus*. A collectively experienced, yet differentially embodied, seasonality was, I argue, a necessary pre-condition for the translation of priestly and chiefly agency into revolutionary social change.

Pre-Christian seasonal rites in eastern Polynesia and Hawai'i were orchestrated by priests in accordance with observed movements of the Pleiades, a beautiful star-cluster in the Taurus constellation. The Pleiades were important to the early, yam-growing, proto-Polynesians who termed this star cluster *matariki*. The cluster continued to be accorded ritual and seasonal significance by the proto-Polynesians' descendants in the eastern Pacific, as *matali'i* (Hawai'i), *matari'i* (Society Islands) or *matariki* (Southern Cook Islands and New Zealand) (Kirch and Green 2001: 261–63). In all of these societies, its heavenly movements heralded two seasons (*tau* or *kau*); the beginning of one was signalled by the (acronitic) rising of the stars above the horizon after sunset in November, the beginning of the other was signalled by either their setting in May or by their brief re-appearance (heliacal rising) before dawn in June (Kirch and Green 2001: 261; Babadzan 1993: 223–33).

William Ellis, a missionary of the London Missionary Society (LMS), records that beyond calculation in terms of generations, the most general divisions of time in Tahiti were by the year (*matahiti*) or by half-yearly seasons, termed *matari'i* after the Pleiades constellation that marked their division (1829b: 418). Pomare referred to these as 'kingly seasons' (*tau ari'i*) emphasizing their ritually-totalizing significance. The season of *matari'i-i-nia* or 'Pleiades above' began in November, while the season of *matari'i-i-raro* or 'Pleiades below' began in May (ibid.: 419; Henry 1928: 332). Within 'Pleiades above' the period from mid-December to mid-January was known as the 'sacred ripening of the year' when the breadfruit ripened heralding a time of plenty (Ellis 1829b: 419–20; Henry 1928: 177; Moerenhout 1983: 260). Hostilities suspended, this was a time for the people and the god, Ro'omatane; it was a time for general feasting, sports, dancing and 'national rejoicing' (Ellis 1829a: 287–92; Moerenhout 1983: 262). Europeans who witnessed these events likened them to what occurred during an English country fair (Wilson 1799: 323; Turner in Henry 1928: 177). While popular, these were, however, essentially religious celebrations, opened by the priest of Ro'omatane and presided over by the gods (Henry 1928: 177, 246; Ellis 1829a: 287–88; Babadzan 1993: 237–40). In direct contrast to the *communitas* during this season of 'Pleiades above', the season of 'Pleiades below' began with rites of hierarchy, termed *pa'iatua*, during which temples were renewed or cleaned and god-images re-wrapped.

The most general division of the Hawaiian year was also between two seasons (*kau*), in this case a wet season and a dry season, both lasting six months (Valeri 1985: 198–99). The year began at the start of the wet season when Pleiades appeared on the horizon in early November. As it did in Tahiti, this season included the rites of *communitas,* here termed *makahiki,* a cognate of the Tahitian word *matahiti*. These centred on the return of the god, Lono, paralleling the return of the Tahitian Ro'omatane. During the dry season, the *luakini* temples, dedicated to the war god Ku, were re-opened with rites directed towards reintegration and hierarchy.

In the Southern Cook Islands of Rarotonga, Aitutaki, Atiu, Ma'uke, Mitiaro and Mangaia, the year was also divided into two *tau* determined by the movements of Pleiades. During the season of Pleiades above, dancing and sporting festivals were held and in Aitutaki (and perhaps elsewhere) a rite termed *pure ari'i* was performed during which chiefs and priests were covered in large amounts of bark-cloth – this was a time for popular celebration free from chiefly surveillance. In contrast, during the season of Pleiades below, rites known as *aka'au takurua* were performed. These included the re-sanctification of temples and processions during which wrapped god-images were paraded around the islands.

Polynesian ritual life did not, of course, run like clockwork. Warfare, the deaths of chiefs, cyclones and other unpredictable events meant that, while the Pleiades oscillation precisely divided the year into two seasons, this division served only as a general guide for ritual action: during the season that began with the rising of Pleiades in November, rites of *communitas* were everywhere performed; during the season that began with the setting or heliacal rising of Pleiades, rites of reintegration were everywhere performed. In the following discussion I detail and compare these contrasting seasonal rites as they were performed in the Society Islands, Hawai'i and the Southern Cook Islands in order to highlight shared features that will take on historical significance in the narrative that unfolds in subsequent chapters of this book. Because my central argument is that the Polynesian Iconoclasm was a regional event that presupposed a shared ritual and seasonal precedent, it is important that I fully describe this precedent. As a ground for historical being, the ritually-produced seasonality of life was fundamental to the indigenous agency through which Christian conversion was effected.

Pleiades Above as a Season of *Communitas*

Writing of the Hawaiian *makahiki,* a festival over which the fertility god, Lono, presided during the season of Pleiades above, Sahlins emphasized that it was a time of '*communitas*', invoking the concept made anthropologically famous by Victor Turner, for whom it was associated with liminality and anti-structure (1989: 395).

The *makahiki* festival had its equivalents in all the societies discussed in this book where episodes of iconoclasm took place, and in all of these societies this annual festival was a time of *communitas,* or, as Durkheim termed it, 'collective effervescence'. In an insightful discussion of Turner's and Durkheim's shared understanding of society and social process, Olaveson concluded that both writers

> saw structure as essentially alienating and posited models whereby it is infused with doses of humanity, intimacy, creativity and equality in the form of effervescent – or *communitas* – laden performances and events. Without a healthy dialectic between collective effervescence/ *communitas* and social structure, social existence could not be. The dialectic constitutes society itself. (Olaveson 2001: 111)

Eastern Polynesian and Hawaiian priests partially shared this scholarly understanding of society. But more importantly, unlike Durkheim and Turner, they practiced it. It was they who initiated the periods of *communitas* by offering sacrifices – in some cases human sacrifices – and it was they who orchestrated the contrasting seasonal rites through which *societas* as hierarchy was re-constituted. They were responsible for reproducing their societies in accordance with a seasonality of life. But their understanding and practice of *communitas* was also distinct from the romanticized version developed by Durkheim and Turner. Polynesian *communitas* included armed conflict and it was often preceded by sacrificial killing.

Jacques Moerenhout, who gained his information in the early 1830s from Tati, a former leading priest of the Papara district of Tahiti, wrote that here human sacrifices were offered as a forerunner to 'horrible amusements' celebrated during the season of Pleiades above (1983: 262). Indeed, missionary journals for the years 1798 to 1808 confirm that human sacrifice, feasting and armed conflicts were the norm for this time of year. On November 17, 1798, for example, LMS missionaries who had arrived in March of the previous year, recorded:

> Several natives are around us with their spears and clubs but peace continues within our dwelling. Hamanemane [the head priest] sent us some hogs etc., perhaps the plunder of our poor neighbours. In the afternoon heard that the priests had returned to Pare where Otu [Tu, later named Pomare] remains to offer up bodies of three men and a child killed this morning in sacrifice to their devil gods. (Missionary Society n.d.: 126)

Two weeks later, the head priest himself would be killed and offered as a sacrifice.

After the offering of human sacrifices, 'grand preparations' were made in all districts of Tahiti, the district chiefs competing with each other to collect the largest offering for the gods. These tributes were taken by canoe to the island's main temple, the King's *marae,* and received on behalf of the King by his priest who had called the canoes on shore. Although a small portion of the offerings were immediately placed on a sacrificial platform (*fata*) for the gods, they were not intended to be shared between the gods and the King as were other tributes. Instead, the people requested the King's portion so that they and the gods should share the offerings, a request that was always consented to. Upon receiving the signal of consent, the multitudes rushed onto the temple court as a disorderly mob to snatch and fight over their portions. Loud noises (trumpets, drumming), disorder and extravagant sartorial display characterized the whole event as the people and the gods took charge. After this mass confusion, the offerings were returned and carefully divided by the priests among the families (Moerenhout 1983: 260–62; Henry 1928: 177).

A description of this rite (known as *parara'a matahiti* or *maoara'a matahiti*), appears to have been given to James Wilson, Captain of the *Duff*, the ship by which the first missionaries were transported to Tahiti in 1797. In an appendix to his narrative of the voyage Wilson described the event as 'sport':

> The things appointed for this sport are all brought together in one open space. The chief's men hold the hogs fast, till the priest has made a long prayer on the occasion: at the conclusion of it he throws a young plantain into one of the canoes, which stand in a row with the masts erected to spread the cloth and hang the bamboos of oil; immediately on this signal the hogs, goats and fowls are let loose and the young men and women begin the chase which continues a considerable time before all are caught: after this the presents are given and the feast served up. Wrestling and dancing occupy a part of every day and night while the feast continues. (Wilson 1799: 323–24)

Following this rite, the priests of all district temples and men at their family temples offered sacrifices to call forth the gods and ancestors from the dark, obscure world of *Po* to *Rotunoanoa*, 'a perfumed place of light and enjoyment' associated with Ro'omatane ('Tane the Voluptuous' in Henry's translation). This god closely corresponds to Lono of Hawai'i and Rongomatane or Rongo of the Southern Cook Islands (Henry 1928: 246). Thus the transition from one season to another had its cosmological parallel in the heavenly travel of divinities (stars included). From *Rotunoanoa* the spirits of ancestors returned with Ro'omatane to spend time with their descendants in the world of the living (Henry 1928: 177; Babadzan 1993: 239). The offerings to the gods at the national *marae* and then at all other *marae* across Tahiti united gods, ancestors and humanity.

So, too, did the sports competitions, the dancing and the feasting, as Handy stresses:

> While superficially the main object in the festivities seems to have been enjoyment, there was certainly an underlying religious meaning. In the first place, just as the offerings at this and other times were intended to attract the gods to places where their presence was desired, so on these occasions of food gathering the feasting, sports and dances were undoubtedly thought and intended to attract the gods, in whose honour the rites were celebrated, to the localities where their influence (*mana*) was needed. The very bounty of the feasts at this time was probably also believed both to strengthen and to exhilarate the gods present as it did men and to affect directly the fecundity of the earth. (Handy 1927: 306–7)

Moerenhout tells us that these same *matahiti* ceremonies took place throughout the Society Islands, however little has been recorded concerning those outside Tahiti (1983: 262). For Huahine, Ellis recorded that while, in general, only men attended major festivals, during the *maoara'a matahiti* a 'sumptuous banquet' was attended by men, women and children. Following the banquet, families departed for their own temples to pray for the spirits of departed relatives to return from the *Po* to *Rotunoanoa* and temporarily inhabit the bodies of the living (1829b: 217–18). Henry added that, as part of the welcome for the spirits of deceased 'friends', some families 'spread out lines of sacred bark-cloth (*tapa*) in their houses' (1928: 177).

The Hawaiian *makahiki* has been described in careful detail by Valeri (1985: 200–33) and Sahlins has provided us with insightful accounts of its historical significance in relation to the death of Cook and subsequent early nineteenth century events (I consider in some detail historical improvisations of the *makahiki* in later chapters). Sahlins has rightly stressed that, in general, the *makahiki* was a *popular* festival that celebrated the 'the eclipse of the established order' (1989: 413). In common with the *matahiti* celebrations in Tahiti, it included revelry and open displays of sexuality, particularly erotic dancing, intended to attract and 'exhilarate' the gods, as Handy put it in the above-quoted passage.

Prior to the main *makahiki* rites, tributary offerings were made by the people to the chiefs. As in Tahiti, each district chief gathered a large amount of tribute, including bark cloth, skirts, loincloths, fish, dogs 'and many other things' (Valeri 1985: 204). These 'riches' were brought to the King and placed before his feathered god to be later distributed among the priests and nobility. However, unlike the Tahitian practice, 'nothing at all' was given to the commoners who produced the goods (Valeri 1985: 204). The *makahiki* rites proper centred on images of the fertility god Lono, these constructed as three different poles: a long god (*akua loa*), a short god (*akua poko*) and a god of games (*akua pa'ani*). The long god had Lono's head carved at one end and a cross-bar, from which were hung feather-wreathes, bird skins and bark cloth. On the evening after these gods had been decorated people drank large quantities of kava and sang blasphemous, cursing songs. Commoners and nobles, men and women, then bathed together in the ocean under the gaze of the *makahiki* images planted in the sand. Over the next four days, sexual orgies and feasting took place, while killing and sacrifices were forbidden. During this period of revelry the high priest was secluded and blindfolded so that he would not see the violations of sacred restriction (Valeri 1985: 205–7).

Lono processions followed. While short gods were taken on tours of districts, the long god was taken on a circuit of each island, stopping at each district boundary where first-fruit sacrifices were presented by the people. These offerings included precious feathers, pigs, bark-cloth, pounded taro and chickens. The long god image was then turned face down and its place was taken by the god of games. Four days of sport and dancing followed, the sport including boxing matches and battles during which people were injured and sometimes killed (Valeri 1985: 207–9; Sahlins 1989: 394–95). Sahlins has suggested that events were intended not to attract the gods but to 'send them away again' (1989: 395), but Handy's view – that they were intended to 'exhilarate' the gods – seems to be a better interpretation. Lono would be sent away later; the King returned from his confinement in the temple to defeat Lono and banish him to Kahiki, the world of ancestors. The images of Lono were then dismantled – Lono had become the first sacrificial victim of a progressively restored order (Valeri: 1985: 211–13).

Little is known about the pre-Christian seasonal rites in the Southern Cook Islands. However, there is strong evidence that here too the year was divided into two seasons, one associated with *communitas* and the other with hierarchy. The most detailed account of pre-Christian ritual in Rarotonga is contained in a collection of Rarotongan traditions written by Te Ariki Tara'are and published, with a translation by S. Percy Smith and Steven Savage, in the *Journal of the Polynesian Society* (Te Ariki-tara-are 1921: 129–41). The relevant section is translated by Savage and titled 'Concerning the Ceremonies and Festivals brought by Tangiia to Rarotonga from Avaiki'. This text proved very difficult to translate, even for Savage, the author of an excellent Rarotongan-English dictionary. To make matters worse, it appeared to Savage that the festivals were not described in any logical sequence but were written down 'as they occurred to the reciter' (Te Ariki-tara-are 1921: 129).

The rites of Pleiades above are described as follows:

> When it came to the month of *erui-tutae-nui* (month of March) this was a time of plenty and the people bedecked the emblems [god images] of the festival of fasting [held in preparation for this festival the month before] with garlands of flowers and then built an immense *karioi* house (in which to sing and dance) and plenty of bruised bread-fruit and over-ripe bread-fruit were eaten by all the people. (Te Ariki-tara-are 1921: 130)

Spear-fighting skills were then dramatically displayed, war songs of challenge and reply were sung and a great feast that included a large number of pigs was served. In preparation for these festivities a large amount of kava was drunk and the gods returned from Avaiki, the world of gods and ancestors, to the world of the living. Savage translates the original passage *Kua muumuu aere Te Atua-tini ki reira* as 'murmurings of the gods were heard', but a more literal translation would be 'The many-gods came quietly to that place'.

While there are no eye-witness accounts of these festivities, we have a good description of related rites observed in neighbouring Aitutaki written by Papeiha, a Raiatean evangelist, in 1821. Papeiha describes the rites as 'a great feast' termed *pure ariʻi* or 'prayers of the high chiefs', that began in late November when the entire population had gathered at the island's main temple. As hierarchy gave way to *communitas,* the chiefs and their families literally concealed themselves from the rest of society: 'the kings or rather the family of the kings take their seats in separate situations from the common people. They cover themselves completely with cloth except a small part of their faces' (Williams n.d.(a): 14). This covering recalls the confinement and blind-folding of the Hawaiian high priest during the *makahiki.* Chiefs remained covered on the *marae* and engaged in prayer while the commoners embarked on a festive tour of their island:

> The people clothe themselves with the finest of their cloth and make a tour round the island. Before they set out they go to the Marae [original caps] and cover the kings with cloth in great abundance. They leave the Marae, everyone with a large piece of wood on his shoulder which they use in the separation of their wrestlers, for when they leave the Marae and make a tour of the island they wrestle in every district. Sometimes there are two or three wrestlings in a district. This finishes the ceremony of bure ariʻi [pure ariʻi]. (ibid.)

No doubt the wrestling was accompanied by dancing, singing and feasting.

The Mangaian year was also divided into two seasons, the first commencing in mid-December when Pleiades appeared on the evening horizon. According to W. W. Gill, a missionary who lived on Mangaia between 1852 and 1872, this was 'everywhere a time of extravagant rejoicing and was welcomed with frantic dances and discordant shell music' (1894: 333n2). Today, each of the six districts of Mangaia participates, separately, in *matahiti* ceremonies marking the New Year. In these ceremonies, food is presented by each family to the district chief (*kavana*) who then proceeds to re-distribute it evenly among the families. This careful re-distribution, which I have witnessed, recalls the division of offerings in Tahiti after they had been snatched by the masses from the temples during the *matahiti* there. In addition to this rite today, each of the church congregations is invited to a feast hosted by a neighbouring congregation, this new-year feasting moving, annually, in a clockwise circuit around the island. It is not certain that these rites have pre-Christian precedents but I think it likely that they do (Rod Dixon, pers. comm.).

In the Society Islands, Hawaiʻi and the Southern Cook Islands then, the period of Pleiades above was one of fertility and abundant life associated with the return of Rongo/Lono from the world of ancestors to the world of the living. It was a time for the joyous reunion of people and gods, people and ancestors. In Hawaiʻi and the Southern Cook Islands the drinking of large quantities of kava at the beginning of this period facilitated the reunion. This uniting of humanity and divinity, ancestors and living descendants, was everywhere expressed as sexual union, vigorous dancing and competitive sports that, in some cases, included high levels of violence. This was *communitas* Polynesian-style.

The fertilizing rites of Pleiades above were also socially totalizing, bringing together whole districts and whole islands. This unification was expressed spatially though the circuits that were made of the islands in Hawai'i, the Southern Cook Islands and the Society Islands. (We shall see in Chapter 5 that circuits of Tahiti were also made by the King at this time.) Only in the Society Islands, it seems, was the beginning of this period marked by human sacrifices. However, initial tributary offerings to the high chiefs featured in all three of the island groups considered here. The distribution of these offerings was also a socially totalizing event, carried out with particular care. In Hawai'i, the practice of only distributing tribute to the gods, the King and the nobility reflected a heightened sense that society was embodied in this grouping alone.

Pleiades Below as a Season of Hierarchy

The revelries of Pleiades above were not suitable for royal or priestly eyes – hence the Hawaiian King was confined to his temple, the Hawaiian priest was blindfolded and in Aitutaki chiefs and priests covered themselves with large quantities of bark cloth. In contrast, many of the rites of Pleiades below were for priestly and chiefly eyes only. Moreover, separation between gods, priests and people, rather than union, was emphasized. Let us now consider these rites in more detail, beginning again in the Society Islands.

The Tahitian season of *matari'i-i-nia* or 'Pleiades above' was followed by that of *matari'i-i-raro* or 'Pleiades below'. The most important rite performed at the beginning of this season was the *pa'iatua* or 'god-wrapping'. This was a dramatic performance through which gods were called to sanctify their images and then sent away, leaving only priests and high chiefs as their representatives in the world of light. The fullest accounts of the *pa'iatua* are those of Teuira Henry (1928: 157–77) and the LMS missionary William Ellis (1829b: 205–6). Henry was the granddaughter of John Orsmond, an LMS missionary in the Society Islands between 1817 and 1856, and her book is a revision of his initial manuscript.

In preparation for the *pa'iatua* rites, priests separated themselves from ordinary (*noa*) life in order to purify themselves for sacred (*ra'a/tapu*) performances during which they would interact closely with their gods. They slept away from their families and avoided touching cooked food which was considered particularly polluting (*noa*). Also in preparation for the events, the priests placed a *ra'ui* (sacred restriction) over the entire island that prohibited activities such as fishing, gardening and the lighting of cooking fires. Commoners had to take particular care not to meet or come into contact with, and thereby contaminate priests and the King. Rites of hierarchy required a strict separation of *tapu* and *noa*.

The royal *marae* was carefully weeded and re-decorated by the King and chiefs and on the following night the priests walked, unseen by the masses, in procession to this temple carrying small wrapped images of messenger gods (*ti'i*). These were unwrapped and symbolically washed before being sent with prayers to fetch the main gods. At dawn the next day 'the most awe-inspiring of all processions' took place, again witnessed only by the participants. The head priest led the procession adorned with a feather headdress. He was followed by four priests who carried, in an ark, the wrapped image of the main god, 'Oro. Behind them, were other priests carrying wrapped images of gods associated with healing, canoe construction and fishing. At the tail of the procession were a class of priests known as *feia tahutahu*. When attached to the royal *marae,* their role was 'to avenge the King and chiefs on their enemies, to annihilate offending *tahutahu* of an inferior order, to destroy national foe and to aid the warrior by performing deadly rites upon slain or captured chiefs in time of war' (Henry 1928: 206). Henry called them 'wizards'. *Feia tahutahu* were also involved in the enforcement of a moral order through the detection and punishment of crimes against the King and gods (ibid.). In the procession they carried small wrapped *ti'i*, probably similar to those used to fetch the gods the night before. As we shall see in Chapter 7, after the Tahitian iconoclasm some of these priests continued to enforce a moral order, although it would now be Christian one, by becoming judges and that some of these judges donned the feather headdresses they had formerly worn in the *pa'iatua* processions.

After the procession had arrived at the *marae,* a ceremony of feather exchange took place. As described by Ellis, wrapped god-images were unwrapped and brought out onto the temple court from the house in which they had been stored. They were then rubbed with scented oils and exposed to the sun. Priests who wished to have the *mana* of their god-images 'recharged' with the *mana* of these larger, more powerful images presented a number of red feathers to the temple priests and, in exchange, received two or three feathers that had been attached to the wrappings of the larger images. The feathers that they had presented to the priests were then attached to the larger images in order that they might absorb their *mana* and be used to recharge smaller gods at the next *pa'iatua* ceremony. The newly feathered, smaller god-images were then placed before the larger gods and a priest prayed that the *mana* from the larger image be transferred to smaller images (Ellis 1829b: 205–6).

Henry's account is in close agreement with that of Ellis, except that she does not mention the anointing of the images with oil. She does, however, provide some additional detail regarding the main god, 'Oro, which she describes as 'lying in state', like the body of a chief:

When the image of the tutelar god ['Oro] was revealed from the pro-
fusion of red and yellow feathers [with which it had been wrapped]
lying upon its coverings on the mat within the *'ava'a* [the most sacred enclosure of the *marae*] the worshippers prostrated themselves
… then followed the presentation of minor gods by their owners in
their proper turns with offerings of new *'ura* [red feather] amulets
and loose feathers which were given through the high priest to the
tutelar god in exchange for some in his possession. This act was called
taritoara'a-atua (the god's exchange) and was supposed to add new
power from the greater god to the lesser ones … the old wrappings
of the images of the tutelar god were removed for new ones and as it
remained uncovered, lying in state with its guests within the *'ava'a*,
a sacrifice [of a pig] called *fei-'au* (petition with food) was offered.
(Henry 1928: 168)

In Chapter 6, I suggest that this renewal of hierarchy through the distribution of feathers charged with the *mana* of 'Oro was a ritual precedent
for improvised new practices of printing and distributing biblical texts that
embodied the words of the new God, Jehova. These texts were initially printed
with priestly assistance on press set up in Mo'orea in 1817 and distributed by
priests to chiefs of Mo'orea and Tahiti.

After the pig-sacrifice, a great drum was sounded as the images were re-
wrapped and returned to their storage house; 'Oro remained in the sacred enclosure. When the drumming stopped a sense of relief spread throughout the
surrounding area because the most sacred part of the rite was now concluded.
Cooking fires would soon be lit throughout the island.

With the god-images now safely re-wrapped a ritual transition from a
symbolic state of *Po* (world of the gods) to *Ao* (the world of light) was made.
Priests chanted, '*Po* is passed, the *Ao* is for the King. Stars, moon and sun are
encircling garlands'. Portions of the creation chant were recited by priests and
chiefs in unison as cosmic order and, with it, chiefly hierarchy were restored.
More pigs were sacrificed and in lieu of human sacrifice a banana shoot, termed
'*ta'ata-o-mei'a-roa*' (man-long-banana) was also offered. 'Oro was then addressed by the King's priest: 'let the priesthood hold the sanctification [*ra'a*] of
the sovereign [*ari'i rahi*] and congregation [*opure*] . . . turn thy face to *Po*, look
not upon the deeds of men'. This prayer initiated the 'grand dismissal' (*pari-
ma-nui*) during which priests and others departed from the temple and 'Oro,
in his ark, was returned to the storage house. The priests urged the gods to 'let
sacredness remain' at the temple so that the participants could become free
(*noa*). As they left the temple and the world of the gods, the priestly and chiefly
members of the congregation placed wreaths on a stone image of Ro'omatane,
saying, 'these are wreaths for thee, godly priest, O Ro'omatane. Wreaths for dis-

missal; let *tapu* remain here. Dismiss us, dismiss us that we may become *noa*'. This was appropriate because Ro'omatane stood, like a priest, at the boundary between the world of gods and ancestors and the world of the living; in order for the spirit of a deceased chief to enter *Rohutunoanoa* it needed to present red feathers to Ro'omatane (Henry 1928: 201).

Drums and trumpets sounded, signalling that people were now free to open the feast ovens. Food, supplemented by mats, rolls of bark cloth and feather ornaments for the god storage-house, was placed in a heap for the priests and gods. Commoners then took their food home where men and women consumed it separately. The priests remained to share the offerings with their gods at a special feast held in a long eating shed near the temple.

According to Moerenhout, these rites began a 'season of mourning or of the departure of the gods' (1983: 259). The revelry of Pleaides above had cele-brated the reunion of people with gods and ancestors:

> And then they have another ceremony which leaves no more doubt about the purpose of these first. It was the celebration of the departure of the gods for their stay with the dead or in obscurity [*Po*]. This cer-emony and the feasts which accompanied it took place in some of the Society Islands and in almost all others [i.e. the Austral Islands]. They went then to the marais [*marae*] and they prayed to the gods to return promptly [at the next rising of Pleiades] from their stay in obscurity or death (Po to Rohoutou noa noa [*Rohutunoanoa*], the abode of light and life). (1983: 252–53)

Building on Henry's observation that the 'Oro image appeared to be 'lying in state', Babadzan (1993; 2003) has provided an insightful interpretation of the *pa'iatua* rites in which he compares them with funeral rites. The exposure of god-images (*to'o*) to the sun and the rubbing of their 'bodies' with scented oil before they were re-wrapped recalled the treatment of a chief's body after death. Like a corpse, the *to'o* thus appeared as a body in relation to a soul (2003: 41). But further to this interpretation, when we view these actions as part of rite that is opposed to the *matahiti* celebrations of Pleiades above, a cosmolog-ical reversal is evident: while, at death, the 'soul' of a chief departed for *Po* (via *Rotunoanoa*) and was later called to return with Ro'omatane during the period of Pleiades above, the 'soul' of the god was called from *Po* to inhabit the *to'o*-body at the beginning of the *pa'iatua* rite and sent back to *Po* at the conclusion of the rite. All this confirms Babadzan's observation that 'the entire ceremony [was] performed as if it were in the power of man, and above all the priests, to gather and disperse the gods, to control and command them' (2003: 44; see also 1993: 126–27).

Moerenhout noted that *pa'iatua* rites were performed in 'some of the So-ciety Islands'. Certainly, these would have included Ra'iatea and Taha'aa, their place of origin, and Tahiti's near neighbour, Moʻorea. Huahine was distinctive, however, because there the equivalent rites centred not on ʻOro, but on Tane. In 1822, a visiting London Missionary Society delegation led by Rev. Tyerman and George Bennett recorded that the image of Tane had been of similar size and shape to that of the Tahitian ʻOro image: 'a huge mis-shapen block of wood' the size of a very tall and stout man wrapped in a sheath of coconut fibre (Tyerman and Bennet 1841: 72). A *paʻiatua*-like ceremony was described to them by the leading priest and recorded as follows:

> At [Tane's] marae, once a year when the King and priests thought proper, there was what might be called a national assembly and festival held. Hither all the idols of Huahine were brought from their various temples to be clothed with new dresses [wrappings] and ornaments. On this occasion Tane was laid on the middle of his bed [a stone platform 24 feet long and 13 feet wide] having the gods of four districts placed on his right hand and the gods of four other districts into which the island was divided on his left. The chiefs stood in rows opposite their own divinities and the priests round Tane, as lord over them all. Various antic ceremonies having been performed and prayers offered, the images were stripped of the old vestments. Many of these wooden stocks, being hollow, were [i.e., had earlier been] filled with beautiful feathers and other trinkets which were also brought out and either renewed or replaced. None but men were allowed to attend this ceremony. (Tyerman and Bennet 1841: 72)

At the conclusion of the rite, a sumptuous feast was served to the participants at which a large amount of kava was consumed. As in Tahiti, cooking fires were prohibited and the usual daily tasks were suspended during the performance of the ceremony.

The LMS authors do not say when this rite was performed but this was almost certainly in May or June, and in direct opposition to the *maoaraʻa matahiti* rites during which, as noted above, deceased relatives were welcomed back with offerings placed on long strips of white bark-cloth inside their houses.

Sahlins contrasted the Hawaiian *makahiki*, as a time of popular rejoicing, of carnival kings (as Lono) and *communitas,* with *societas,* social order in general as it existed throughout the rest of the year (1989: 395). As a priestly-orchestrated festival or rite, however, it contrasted most strongly with priestly controlled rites of *hierarchy* that were staged in May and June after the building, re-building or renovation of temples dedicated to the King's god, Ku. Although on a grander scale than the *paʻiatua* rites, these *luakini* rites were clearly closely related to them. Handy speculated that the Hawaiian *makihiki* rites originated in Tahiti – 'the presentation of first fruits in Hawaiʻi may be said to have been correlated with the Tahitian season and the use of breadfruit as a staple while it had no particular connection with the harvesting of taro' (1927: 302). We might also speculate that the opposing rites of hierarchy had the same point of origin. The following account of these *luakini* rites highlights features that had parallels in the *pa'iatua*.

We have seen that in preparation for the *pa'iatua* rites the Tahitian *marae* were meticulously weeded and decorated with flowers and the whole island was declared *tapu*, with no cooking fires being permitted. Similarly, in Hawai'i at the time when the *luakini* temples were built or rebuilt, the whole island was purified. Specifically, the road around the island was cleared of weeds 'from one end to the other', and each person who had land adjacent to the road contributed to this activity (Malo 1951: 163). Like the Tahitian rites, those within the *luakini* were performed and witnessed solely by priests and chiefs and they, like those in the Society Islands, also needed to be purified before participating in the main rites. In Hawai'i, these rites of purification, collectively termed *huikala*, included a ceremony in which priests performed a sequence of rites of self-consecration, each in a different temporary hut, these immediately made *noa* (free from *tapu*) after the rites had been performed in them (ibid.). In general, the rites of separation between *tapu* participants and a relatively *noa* population were more highly elaborated in Hawai'i than in Tahiti.

A dramatic feature of the Tahitian *pa'iatua* was a strictly ordered procession of priests carrying god-images to the *marae*. The Hawaiian equivalent was the *kauila nui* or *kauila huluhulu* rite (Malo 1951: 167; Valeri 1985: 269). Unlike that of Tahiti, however, the beginning of this procession was witnessed by the masses who were seated in rows outside the temple. As recalled by Malo:

> Then the keepers of the *kaai* gods [portable gods on top of poles] came, each one bearing the *kaai* god of his chief (the *kaai* god of the king [Ku] also was there). The number of these idols was very great. The god Kahoalii, also, was impersonated by a man in a state of nudity. At this juncture, the *kaai* gods being held aloft, each on his spear decorated with a banner, the [keeper] of each sat in front to the god of his charge waiting for the signal to run in a circle about all the *kaai* gods. (1951: 167)

After proceeding into the temple the king and nobility were seated in rows (probably reflecting rank) and instructed by a priest to remain silent. The gods were then paraded within the temple led by the naked representative of Kahoalii referred to by Malo in the above passage (Valeri 1985: 281–85).

These feather gods, more generally termed *akua hulu manu*, were images consisting of a head made from wicker (split aerial roots of *'ie'ie*) and covered with sacred red and yellow feathers. They were housed in the *mana* house (*hale mana*) at the sacred heart of the *luakini*. Valeri tells us that these mobile images 'follow[ed] the king and nobles everywhere they [went] to wage war, to meet their peers in ceremony … or to perform rituals' (ibid.: 247). Other images stored in the *hale mana* were wooden figures. Surviving early-nineteenth-century images from the island of Hawai'i are between a metre and two-and-a-half metres tall. They are characterized by a crouching posture, an immense mouth full of teeth apparently ready to devour, a headdress and elongated eyes.

It appears that, as in the *pa'iatua,* the feathers on the god-images were renewed during these *luakini* rites. Prior to the temple performances 'the people of each land (*'aina*) in successive order' had brought tribute (*ho'okupu*) to the King, including pigs, food cloth and, most ritually significant, feathers. These were subsequently used to revive the images and imbue them 'with divine presence' (Valeri 1985: 257, 270). Valeri added:

> Moreover, these feathers went first to the King and his god as representatives of Ku in his general form. Now the King redistributes them among his nobles so that they may revivify the particular forms of the god associated with them. Hence the 'downward' movement of the feathers from King to nobles parallels the 'downward' movement of Ku from his generic to specific forms. (ibid.)

The parallels with the *pa'iatua* rite of the Society Islands are striking.

The *Luakini* rites concluded with sacrifices, the presentation of offerings to priests and feasting. A large number of pigs provided by the nobles were cooked and one of the fore-quarters of each was given to the priests. The King then offered the gods a great sacrifice consisting of four hundred of each – pigs, bananas, coconuts, red fish and bundles of cloth – and some human victims:

> Then the King comes out of the temple to give some pork to the feather gods, to the priests, to the ali'i and all the people of distinction … Each receives a share according to his rank. The crowd of 'very little people' (kanaka li'ili'i loa) also receive their share after that of the king has been cooked. Moreover, about two hundred hogs are allotted to the temple's 'wooded gods'. (Valeri 1985: 311)

The strict separation that had been in force between chiefs and commoners could now be relaxed as 'all the people, priests, chiefs and commoners went to bathe in the ocean' (Malo 1951: 175).

The re-wrapping of images was central to the *pa'iatua,* this reflected in the name of the rite which, as already noted, literally translates as 'god-wrapping'. Wrapping also featured at different stages of the *luakini* rites (Valeri 1985: 300–2, 396n177). Malo wrote that the images paraded in the temple were, like the god who led them, naked (1951: 169). It was only later, after the great sacrifice, that each was wrapped in a white loin-cloth (*malo*) (ibid.: 173–74). Prior to this wrapping, the four posts of the god-house (*hale mana*) were bound with sacred cord and its rafters wrapped with sennit and bundles of sacred bark-cloth (ibid.: 171). Finally, the temple (*heiau*) itself, represented by an image of a god installed at the beginning of the rites, was wrapped:

> All the female chiefs, relations of the king, came to the temple bring-
> ing a *malo* of great length as their present to the [temple] idol … One
> end of the *malo* was borne into the *heiau* (being held by priests) while
> the women chiefs kept hold of the other end. (ibid.: 175)

In both Tahiti and Hawai'i, then, the renewal of hierarchy entailed the renewal and wrapping of god-images. In an important rethinking of the wrapping of images in the Society Islands and elsewhere in east Polynesia, Adrienne Kaeppler has suggested that the feather, sennit and bark-cloth coverings were in fact more significant and sacred than the images themselves (2007). The wrapping of male images with bark-cloth and sennit made by chiefly women incited potency in the images, invigorating them while, at the same time, placing them under priestly control. The gods could now depart leaving behind the king and his priests as their representatives.

Turning, finally, to the Southern Cook Islands, it appears from Tara'are's account that the Rarotongan festivities of Pleiades below, through which the gods were sent away and hierarchy was restored, also strongly contrasted with rites of Pleiades above. In Rarotonga, in the month of May, during a period known as *aka'au ariki* (establishing the peaceful rule of the high chiefs) messengers were sent around the island by the priests calling on people to prepare for the *aka'au takurua* rites (Te Ariki-tara-are 1921: 138). The rites began in a similar way to those of the *pa'iatua* and *luakini*: The road around the island was cleaned, the *marae* were weeded and 'god-posts' (possibly poles on the *marae* or the posts of the god-house) were decorated with flowers. A sequence of priestly and chiefly processions was then staged. While there are no available descriptions of these processions the Tara'are text includes a legendary account of the first *aka'au takurua* performed for the founding ancestor, Tangiia and directed by his priest. The following account of these processions is based on the original Tara'are text (ibid.: 138–40) rather than on Savage's very loose translation.

At the head of the first legendary procession was an assembly of gods. They were followed by dancers performing mourning dances (*eva-tipa*), ones appropriate to a rite which preceded the departure of the gods. Behind them came people carrying offerings for the gods. Stopping at a *marae* near the sea, the gods drank chiefly kava – kava oozed over their skin. The procession then entered the sea where the gods splashed water on their heads to purify themselves. When the procession left the sea Tangiia, the founding ancestor, and his gods led the way onto the shore followed by the other gods. All then feasted.

If this legendary procession was re-enacted then it is possible that priests carried unwrapped staff gods to the coast in order to purify them with seawater. Rarotongan staff-gods were long poles, up to 20 feet in length, with a carved figure at one end (the 'head') and a carved phallus at the other. Normally wrapped in many metres of bark-cloth, they were so heavy that a group of people was needed to carry one of them. The LMS missionary, John Williams, wrote that he was presented with fourteen of these 'immense idols' in 1827 and that they were unwrapped in his presence (Williams 1839: 116). We might further speculate that after the procession of images had reached the main temple, the priests, on behalf of their gods, drank kava and ritually cleansed themselves in the sea.

On the second day of Tangiia's legendary *aka'au takurua*, offerings were made on all the temples to honour the gods (ibid.: 140). On the third day the head priest instructed people how to perform a number of other processions, the last of which was a rite of unity and hierarchy termed *aka moe rakau* or 'putting staffs to sleep'. Here is Savage's rather free translation of the difficult passage:

> As each party moved on to take their place or part in the ceremony each performer followed directly behind the man in front to him, the rule to be observed was that each man stepped in the footmark of the one who went before him in a direct line behind the leader and encircled a fire (a fire that had been made for the purpose and which was not allowed to go out). Ka'ukura [a god] and the company of gods formed the inner circle and when each had attained their appointed place they cast down their staffs or spears [*rakau*] alongside the fire. In making the circle round the fire each one had to stop in time, no-one was to make a mis-step. (Te Ariki-tara-are 1921: 133)

Two processions of dancers followed, each of which formed a circle outside the one before at the fire; 'thus party after party joined in the ceremony until the signal was given to retire'. In breaking up the circles the mourning dancers (*eva-tipa*) who had formed the last circle led the way at the head of a continuous line:

> Those who brought up the rear [the inner-most circle of gods] had to remain standing on the road [near the main *marae*] at Tupapa, hence the saying 'out of action, they stood upon the great road at Tupapa'. (ibid.: 134)

This ceremony appears to have enacted a departure of the gods, these led away by mourning dancers and left 'out of action'. In my view, it is likely that in the ritual re-enactment the *rakau* laid down in front of the fire by the inner circle were staff-gods (*atua rakau*) laid down by their priests. In Tahiti, the gods were urged to depart for *Po* and perhaps a similar separation from the gods was enacted here by putting the wrapped wooden images (*rakau*) to sleep (*akamoe*). But it is also possible that they were spears (as Savage suggests in his translation) and that this was a ritual performance to establish a peaceful hierarchy.

Like the *pa'iatua* and *luakini* rites, the *aka'au takurua* was clearly a total-izing rite of hierarchy. Tangiia, who is said to have brought the rite to Raro-tonga from the abode of the gods in Avaiki, established a total social order by making a circuit of the island and consecrating temples as he went. These were connected by a great ancestral road, the *ara-metua*, which also connected local temples to Arai-te-Tonga, the Royal Court at Tupapa. It was upon this road that the gods were left standing. In preparation for the *aka'au takurua* rite this ritual circuit was re-opened: the temples were cleaned and decorated (proba-bly along with the road that linked them, as in Hawai'i). The priestly and godly processions, which contrasted strongly with the festivities of Pleiades above, were staged on this renewed circuit to restore Tangiia's original hierarchical order, centred on the Royal Court at Tupapa.

Takurua rites were also performed in the southern Cook Islands of Aitut-aki, Atiu, Ma'uke and Mitiaro. However, no details of these performances have been recorded. Williams noted that in Aitutaki, around May or June, there would normally have been a ceremony 'of great pomp' for the 'installation of the king', this contrasting with the *pure ari'i* festivities of Pleiades above (Wil-liams n.d.(a): 44). In July, 1823, when Williams visited Atiu, Ma'uke and Mi-tiaro, people were preparing for *takurua* ceremonies through which the chief of Atiu, Rongomatane, was to be installed as paramount leader for all three islands (Williams 1839: 88–89).

It is likely that Mangaian rites of hierarchy were also performed at the beginning of the season of Pleiades below. When Williams visited Mangaia, in July 1823, people were preparing to inaugurate the reign of a new high chief (*mangaia*) with 'the beating of the *pa'u 'aka'au* drum of peace' (Reilly 2003: 84). It is also certain that the Mangaian chiefly hierarchy closely associated itself with Pleiades. Mangaia, the 'fish of Rongo', was (and remains) divided into six districts corresponding to the six visible stars of Pleiades (Henry 1995: 5–7; Gill 1876: 43). When a new high chief ('temporal Lord') was installed after a period of war, six processions were made around the island. Six layers of Rongo's sacred bark-cloth (*tikoru*) were wrapped around the high-priest of Rongo during his installation rite (Buck 1934: 117). While Gill, in his exten-sive writings on the history of Mangaia, does not describe an equivalent to the *pa'iatua* or *aka'au takurua* rites, curiously, he does append a note on the timing of the appearance and disappearance of Pleiades to an account of the feeding of god-images by a priest and the renewal of their wrappings (1894: 333n2). The account itself, however, emphasizes a contrast between day and night. Twelve (twice six) Mangaiian god-images were kept in a god-house and fed daily by a priest. A triton shell, representing Rongo, was placed at the entrance to the house:

> The entire family of gods was fed before the sun had actually sunk beneath the horizon as that was the signal for them to go on their travels all over the island. At break of day they were said to rush back with a great noise 'like wind in a coconut grove' ashamed of daylight! [The note on Pleiades was inserted here]. Occasionally, the idols were sunned to prevent their fine wrappings from getting mouldy. New white cloth [*tikoru*] was put on them from time to time. (Gill 1894: 333; emphasis added)

This account suggests that the gods did not depart with the disappearance of Pleiades, but remained a constant nocturnal presence. But if this was so, Gill's note on the movements of Pleiades would have no relevance to the feeding and wrapping of the gods and the divine travels he described. The re-wrapping of images with *tikoru* that occurred 'from time to time' was probably linked to the movement of Pleiades.

In all of the societies considered here, the period of Pleiades above was characterized by a union of contraries: *tapu* and *noa,* male and female, chiefs and commoners. In contrast, the period of Pleiades below began with re-assertions of separation. The priests separated themselves from the wider society in order to purify themselves for rites performed in separated, sacred spaces, these also re-consecrated for the event. In the Society Islands the collective gods were brought together in order to be sent away by their priests. In the Southern Cook Islands too, it appears that the gods were separated from people and rendered 'out of action' at this time.

Hierarchy and precedence were everywhere displayed through strictly ordered processions to and within temples, staged to mark transitions from one state of society to another. While most of the population did not participate in these processions (and in the Society Islands they were even prohibited from even viewing them), they did play a central role in staging the events: It was through the gift of their labour that the temples were built or re-built, this labour signalling popular recognition of the hierarchical order put in place.

In the chapters which follow, the shared seasonality of *communitas* and hierarchy described here will assume revolutionary significance as we see it structure the orchestration of a regional event, the Polynesian Iconoclasm and its aftermath. During the season of Pleiades above, when sacrifices had heralded a time of *communitas*, god-images and temples were destroyed or desecrated in the Society Islands, Hawai'i, the Cook Islands and probably two of the Austral Islands. During the season of Pleiades below, when *marae* and *luakini* had been cleaned, built or rebuilt for rites of hierarchy, large chiefly churches were constructed and Biblically-justified laws were proclaimed. Throughout the region, within ten years of these events, rebellions against the new Christian hierarchies were staged. This was again in accordance with the seasonality of life described here – they took place during the period of Pleiades above at a time when society had previously been rejuvenated with revelry.

The seasonality of political life was embodied in differentiated forms of collective *habitus*. Ritual cycles, work cycles, entertainments, feasting and other collective activities assumed and reinforced a concordance of these seasonally-adjusted dispositions. The orchestration of the Polynesian Iconoclasm would also require such a concordance. It is to this regional iconoclasm that I now turn.

❧ 2
The Mo'orean Iconoclasm

Pleiades had just dipped below the evening horizon in June 1815, signalling the beginning of the chiefly season of *matari'i-i-raro,* when Pomare began his circuit of the island of Mo'orea. His party of Christian chiefs and priests included Pati'i, the head priest of Mo'orea who had thrown his god-image onto a large fire some four months earlier. This tour was critical to the realization of Pomare's totalizing ambitions, its main purpose being to secure the ritual and military allegiance of Mo'orean chiefs and priests to himself and his new god, Jehova, prior to his return to Tahiti. In place of the *pa'iatua* rite through which allegiance to Pomare would normally have been enacted, the district chiefs and their priests were invited to participate in its negation, a totalizing sacrifice of their gods to Jehova. They were invited to burn their images and temple structures, and to hold collective feasts at which chiefs and commoners, men and women would eat together. Thus, the Mo'orean iconoclasm unfolded as a series of improvised rituopractical performances that would become the precedent for the wider Society Islands event. In this chapter I describe and analyse this first iconoclasm, and in the next chapter I consider the wider Society Islands event of which this was the initial episode. I begin by sketching the ritual and historical context of Pomare's exile in Mo'orea and I then turn to events that took place during the period 1812–1815. This critical period in Society Islands history began with Pomare's decision to abandon his god, 'Oro, in favor of Jehova. The period culminated with the Mo'orean Iconoclasm.

Ra'iatean Priestly Centrality

Religious conversion was hardly new to the Society Islands. When missionaries from the London Missionary Society (LMS) began preaching there in 1797, Ra'iatean priests had, for at least three decades, been expanding the centralizing influence of their god, 'Oro. Indeed, Babadzan has proposed that conversions to 'Oro were as radical as conversions to Jehova; rather than different chiefly gods occupying the top positions in local cosmological hierarchies, 'Oro became the god of all chiefs, subsuming local hierarchies under him' (1993: 14, my translation). In honour of their new god, Tahitian and Mo'orean 'converts' had built a grand temple, Taputapuatea, named after 'Oro's temple in Ra'iatea (see Figure 2.1). Ra'iatean priestly tradition affirmed the ritual centrality of 'Oro's original temple by speaking of Tahiti as a fish that had broken away from Ra'iatea:

> Tahiti torn away!
> Great plebeian Tahiti
> Great boastful Tahiti
> Grand heedless Tahiti
> Disobedient Tahiti
> Grand capricious Tahiti
> Tahiti of insinuating voice
> O little Tahiti standing on the border
> Mo'orea with eight radiations
> Those art also a part of our fish
> A fish of ours is Tahiti
> Yellow feathers may abound with you
> But red feathers we have in abundance
> (Henry 1928: 436)

Red feathers were more valuable than yellow feathers (although both were closely associated with 'Oro). As we have seen, red feathers were distributed to chiefs during the *pa'iatua* rites in a renewal of centralized hierarchy. Ra'iatea had more red feathers than Tahiti, hence more *mana*. Tahiti and neighbouring Mo'orea were said to be the more common parts of a chiefly fish.

Ra'iatean and Rarotongan traditions were in agreement that, like Tahiti and Mo'orea, Rarotonga had also broken away from Ra'iatea. The LMS missionary John Williams was told by a Ra'iatean priest, sometime between 1816 and 1823, that Rarotongans had made a large drum named Tai-moana or 'Sounder of the Ocean' and this was brought by two priests to Taputapuatea, 'Oro's temple at Opoa in Ra'iatea. For reasons which the narrator did not divulge, both priests were murdered, which so enraged the gods that they lifted up the southern part of Ra'iatea and re-located it as an island somewhere to the south. According to Williams, this tradition convinced him of the existence of Rarotonga before he found it in July 1823. Faaori, a Ra'iatean who accompanied Williams on part of his voyage to Rarotonga, was asked by some Rarotongans, probably priests, why their two drum-bearing ancestors had been killed, thus causing the gods to move their island to its present location. Furthermore, they wanted to know what the Ra'iateans had done with their sacred drum, Tai-moana. Williams was convinced by this exchange and by the knowledge that Rarotongans had of Ra'iatea that 'at some former period more frequent communication must have existed between the islanders' (Williams 1839: 104 and see footnote on p. 104).

Figure 2.1. Taputapuatea *marae,* Ra'iatea. Photo by Hugo Sissons.

Henry records traditions of such communication, although these perhaps speak more reliably of the increasing ritual centrality of Taputapuatea temple within the Society Islands than of links beyond (1928: 119–26). 'Oro is said to have been born at Opoa in Ra'iatea and his father, Ta'aroa, is said to have given him Taputapuatea temple as his home. The image of 'Oro attended by priests at this temple was made from fine sennit (braided coconut fibre) woven into the shape of a man, two or three feet long. Red and yellow feathers were attached to the outside of the image and a chiefly girdle of red feathers was wrapped around it (Henry 1928: 121). As keepers of 'Oro's image in his place of birth, the Ra'iatean priests understood themselves to be at the ritual centre of the world.

A Ra'iatean tradition tells, for example, of a Rarotongan high chief who established a temple adjacent to Taputapuatea at Opoa using a stone from his Rarotongan temple to form the corner-stone of his new one (ibid.: 121). Priests from throughout the region were said to have met periodically in a gathering of 'awful solemnity' at Taputapuatea, where they performed a gigantic regional *pa'iatua*:

> While the mystic rites were being performed that day by the priests
> at the *marae* at Opoa, no fire was kindled and no food was eaten.

When all those who were not of the clergy had retired to the *fare-'opu-nui* (house of august stomachs) and to the *fare-tara-toa* (house of all wisdom), the priests from abroad carefully took their idols, closely covered in choice *tapa* and gay feathers, with offerings for 'Oro in his home and accompanied the priests of the land, also carrying gifts, up into the *marae*. The presiding high priest, the primates and other high priests entered the inner sanctum; the greater body of priests took their places according to their respective ranks upon the walls and outer borders of the *marae*. Then was performed the most sacred of all sacredotal rites, the *pai-atua* (assembly of gods) when it would have meant death for any of the laity to have approached or looked on. (Henry 1928: 125)

According to traditions related by the Mo'orean head priest, Pati'i, the first Tahitian temple for 'Oro was located at Taiarapu, at the head of the fish. Like the Opoa temple, it was also named Taputapuatea and incorporated a stone from the former as a corner-stone. The 'Oro image was:

A small log of *toa* or *aito* (also meaning warrior) about six feet long which was decked in sennit and red, yellow and black feathers to give it all the original attributes of the terrible god. Soon, during the usual solemnities of the occasion, came a strong south-easterly wind, on which 'Oro rode with flashes of lightening. He entered into the image, which was then called 'Oro-rahi-to'o-toa (Great-'Oro-of-the-toa-image), and thus his hold on Tahiti commenced. (ibid.: 130)

Oliver dates the beginning of 'Oro's influence in Tahiti to the middle of the eighteenth century (1974: 1214). Much of the political history of Tahiti and Mo'orea between this time and Pomare's conversion to Christianity in 1812 centres on attempts by various leaders and their priests to assert centrality by gaining ritual control over 'Oro images. In the early 1790s, after Pomare's father had subjugated Mo'orea with the assistance of guns from the *Bounty*, he had a 'splendid' *marae* built in the Papara district of Tahiti. All of Tahiti and Mo'orea, aided by allies from Ra'iatea and the Tuamotu Islands, are said to have contributed to its construction. However, when Ra'iatean priests discovered that Tahitian priests intended to dedicate the temple not to 'Oro but to local gods, they and most of their people departed in anger: 'the very ocean became so agitated that the canoes of the Ra'iateans got swamped at sea in going home' (ibid.: 138). The temple was still unconsecrated when LMS missionaries landed in Tahiti in 1797. Although the names of the god or gods that were to be substituted for 'Oro are not recorded, the incident strongly suggests that certain Tahitian priests had, prior to the arrival of missionaries, been seeking to regain their former independence from Ra'iatea.

Pomare's Jehova Strategy

Rather than adopt his priests' strategy of challenging 'Oro's ritual centrality, Pomare sought, after the death of his father in 1803, to establish himself as *ari'i rahi* (high chief) in Tahiti and Mo'orea through building and strengthening alliances with 'Oro chiefs and priests in the Leeward Islands. One tactic in his push for control was the temporary removal of the 'Oro image from Tautira in Tahiti to the adjacent island of Mo'orea in 1804 and a subsequent reinstallation of the image at Tautira with great ceremony in 1806. Following the return of 'Oro to Tahiti, Pomare redistributed lands and chiefly titles amongst his allies (Oliver 1974: 1316–17). However, Pomare's reign was to prove short-lived. In 1809, after an excessively brutal attempt to enforce his new order, Pomare was forced to flee Tahiti and take up residence in Mo'orea.

LMS missionaries who, for the past twelve years, had made almost no headway in gaining converts, fled at this time, frustrated and fearful, firstly to Huahine and then to Sydney. However, one missionary, Henry Nott, remained with Pomare at Mo'orea, and as the relationship between the two men strengthened so too did Pomare's interest in the political possibilities of Christianity. At Tahiti, a picture of King George that had been sent to Pomare from England was ritually offered to 'Oro. This picture perhaps served as a substitute for Pomare, whose position and that of his father had owed much to English recognition and support. The district and sub-district boundaries of the late eighteenth century were subsequently restored (Oliver 1974: 1335; Davies 1961: 96–136).

In October 1810, there arrived in Mo'orea a future son-in-law and chiefly ally of Pomare from the Leeward island of Borabora named Tapoa, whom one missionary described as the Bonaparte of the South Pacific (Williams 1839: 61). He brought with him, transported in a sacred canoe, a second duplicate of the Ra'iatean 'Oro image. Pomare, Tapoa and their warriors accompanied this image to the Tautira district of Tahiti where they installed the image with elaborate ceremony, as had been done four years previously. Feasting took place throughout Tahiti for months afterwards (Davies 1961: 136–38). But Pomare was again unable to establish his ritual centrality, opposition coming most strongly from Opufara, the *ari'i* of the Papara District. Pomare's 'Oro strategies had been unsuccessful and it was time to contemplate more seriously a Jehova strategy.

Missionaries and their families returned to Mo'orea in 1811 and early 1812 (Davies 1961: 147–53). By this time, Pomare had already decided that he had a better chance of uniting Tahiti and Mo'orea under Jehova than under 'Oro. In local oral tradition, the incident that was most directly associated with this decision was Pomare's refusal to sacrifice a turtle, a chiefly food always shared with gods. A visiting LMS delegation from London led by Tyerman and Ben-

Pomare

Po-ma-re, King of Tahiti, Eimeo, &c.

H. Fisher, Son & C?. London, 1829

Figure 2.2. Pomare. *Source:* Engraving from Ellis (1829a). Victoria University of Wellington.

net was told about Pomare's heroic act some years later in 1821, and they included a brief description of it in their published report:

> On a certain time, a turtle being brought to Pomare he commended
> it to be dressed at his own house and forbade any portion of it to be
> presented at the temple. He then sat down with his household, but no-
> one except himself had the hardihood to taste. (Tyerman and Bennet
> 1841: 24)

Other versions of this incident were recorded by Ellis (1834 II: 93–94) and
Moerenhout (1983: 547), the latter possibly based on versions by Ellis or the
LMS delegation. However, Moerenhout added that the refusal to sacrifice the
turtle occurred 'during a kind of festival'. It is likely that the event occurred in
May or June and hence that the 'kind of festival' referred to by Moerenhout
was a *pa'iatua*. Pomare refused to participate in *marae* sacrifices from mid
1812 onwards (Davies 1961: 159) and so it is possible that this incident signalled his intention not to participate in the *pa'iatua* that marked the beginning of Pleiades below in that year.

Then, in July, 1812, Pomare publicly declared his allegiance to Jehova (Davies 1961: 153). Ellis added:

> At the time that the King thus publicly desired to profess Christianity
> he proposed to erect a large and substantial building for the worship
> of the true God … This island, the Missionaries considered only as a
> temporary residence till they should be able to resume their labours
> in Tahiti, or establish a mission in the Leeward Islands and therefore
> recommended him to defer it. But he replied, 'No, let us not mind
> these things, let it be built.' (1834 II: 95)

In the end, construction work was delayed by fears of war and Pomare's
almost immediate departure for Tahiti where he sought, unsuccessfully, to win
over the Tahitian chiefs to his new god (Davies 1961: 158–59). The chapel was
eventually completed a year later in July 1813.

At the opening service for the new chapel, thirty-one people, most of
whom were from Tahiti and the Leeward Islands, asked that their names be
'written down' by the missionaries as 'professed worshippers of Jehova' (ibid.:
161, 164). This group became known as the *Bure Atua* (God-praying People).
By the time Pomare added his name to the register, in January 1815, its mem-
bership had increased to around four hundred. The majority of these *Bure
Atua* were priests and chiefs. These included Pahi, the head priest of Ra'iatea;
Matapuupuu, the head priest of Huahine; Tati, the head priest of Tahiti's Papara District; Tamatoa, the high chief of Ra'iatea; Utami, the high chief of
Taha'a; the son of the Huahine high chief, Mahine; most of the other Leeward

Island chiefs; and, of course, Pomare himself (Ellis 1834 II: 107; *Quarterly Review* 1830: 10; Davies 1961: 172, 173n4, 182–83).

Following Pomare's lead, these priestly and chiefly members of the *Bure Atua* had abandoned sacrifices on *marae* (see Figure 2.3). Men no longer asserted a privileged relationship with divinity through sharing food with their gods (as offerings), but instead ate with their wives and sisters, thus rendering themselves *noa*, free from *tapu*. In doing so, they paid particular attention to their prayers asking for Jehova's blessing on their food (Ellis 1834 II: 123–25; Davies 1961: 174, 182). Frequent prayer-meetings were held in public and in their homes and they were 'exact in their observance of the Sabbath'.

Sacrifices became public occasions for oppositional performances directed by members of the *Bure Atua* at other chiefs and priests in an attempt to bring them into Pomare's alliance. During a ceremonial presentation of food and cloth to Pomare's sister-in-law, Pomare-Vahine, in March 1815, Farefau, a *Bure Atua* from Borabora loudly and publicly thanked Jehova for providing the food, thus preventing it being offered on the *marae*:

> On such occasions it was customary for a priest or priests to attend; and before any part of it was eaten, to offer the whole to the gods by taking parts of animals and particular kinds of fruit to the temple and depositing them on the altar. The King [Pomare] and his friends [*Bure Atua*] were desirous on this occasion to prevent such acknowledgement. When, therefore, the food was presented to Pomare-Vahine ... one of the principal men [Farefau] who was a Christian came forward, uncovered his head and looking up to the heavens offered in an audible voice their acknowledgment and thanksgivings to Jehova, who liberally gave them food and raiment and every earthly blessing ... no one dared take any part of it to the idol temple. (*Quarterly Review* 1830: 14; Davies 1961: 186)

Two months later, in May, Pomare-Vahine and her sister sailed to Tahiti in an attempt to convince chiefs and priests there to give their allegiance to Pomare and his new god. In Pomare's home district of Pare a large ceremony, probably a *pa'iatua* rite, was staged. As we have seen, this rite included an exchange of feathers, in which those removed from the god-images were presented to chiefs in return for new ones to be attached to the re-wrapped images. On this occasion Farefau's challenge to the priests was more direct than his earlier prayer to Jehova: running towards the officiating priests, he grabbed some bunches of red feathers that had just been removed from the images and threw them into a fire – probably a cooking fire (Ellis 1834 II: 137; Moerenhout 1983: 514). This was viewed as an extremely hostile act, so much so that an attempt was made to massacre Pomare-Vahine's party in the night, forcing them to flee back to Mo'orea (Ellis 1834 II: 139–40; Moerenhout 1983: 514–15).

Figure 2.3. A *marae* at Atehuru, Tahiti. *Source:* Engraving from Wilson (1799). Victoria University of Wellington.

Prelude to Iconoclasm

At the beginning of this year, 1815, when Pomare added his name to the *Bure Atua* register, none of the chiefs or priests of Mo'orea had joined this group and consequently the general population of Mo'orea expressed no interest in becoming members (Davies 1961: 183). The rituopraxis of Pati'i, head priest of Mo'orea would dramatically change this situation, opening the way for the Mo'orean iconoclasm that followed soon after.

The missionaries succinctly reported the sequence of events as follows:

The priest of Papetoai, the District where we reside, renounced heathenism, joined us and publickly [*sic*] committed his god to the flames, others followed his example both here and at Tahiti. (Bicknell and Missionaries to LMS, 5 Sept 1815, SSL)

The only other eyewitness account of the priest's performance was supplied by Davies:

Feby 14th: Pati'i the priest of Papetoai attended the evening meeting and *declared publicly* that he knew well the old religion, had examined it thoroughly and could find no good part in it at all, he had also examined this new Religion [*sic*], every part of it, and could find none bad, it was all good, therefore *he embraced it and renounced the other altogether.* And some time afterwards he took his god and publicly committed it to the flames. (Davies 1961: 184; emphasis added)

William Ellis did not arrive in Moʻorea until 1817 and so his much longer account of the event needs to be treated with caution. He wrote that the preaching of fellow missionary, Henry Nott, had convinced Patiʻi to burn his idols (plural) and that he did so the day after a meeting at which Nott had preached:

After the conclusion of the service he [Patiʻi] and Mr Nott proceeded together along the beach towards the [missionary] settlement. As they walked, Patiʻi fully disclosed the feelings of his mind to Mr Nott and assured him that on the morrow, at a certain hour, he would *bring out the idols* under his care and publicly burn them. (Ellis 1834 II: 109; emphasis added)

It appears from this account that Patiʻi had publicly declared for Jehova at Nott's meeting and had subsequently revealed to the missionary, as they walked home, the dramatic way in which he would follow this up.

Ellis goes on to describe an atmosphere of 'unusual agitation and excitement of feeling' on the day after the beach walk as Patiʻi and his assistants built a large fire adjacent to the main temple. 'Multitudes' assembled and the missionaries are said to have feared the 'tumult [of] devastation and bloodshed' that might follow (ibid.: 110). As the sun set, Patiʻi ordered the fire to be lit and he brought forth his 'idols' from the 'sacred depository of his gods', the *fare-ia-manaha,* and laid them on the ground. Here is the final scene as Ellis imagined it:

Patiʻi tore off the sacred cloth in which they [the images] were enveloped to be safe from the gaze of vulgar eyes; stripped them of their ornaments [feathers] which he cast into the fire; and then one by one threw the idols themselves into the crackling flames – sometimes pronouncing the name and pedigree of the idol and expressing his own regret at having worshipped it – at others, calling upon the spectators to behold their inability to protect themselves. Thus were the idols of which Patiʻi, who was a powerful priest in Eimeo [Moʻorea] had worshipped, publicly destroyed. (ibid.: 112)

The visiting LMS delegation imagined the event somewhat differently in their 1831 report. Here Patiʻi is said to have carried three large idols on his back from the temple to where the fire was burning. Dumping them onto the ground, he is said to have taken an axe and hacked through their sennit wrappings. He then

> split the uncouth shapes to see what might be within, when bones of fishes and men that had been sacrificed were found in the cavities. The dumb logs and stocks were then cast into the flames of a large fire and presently consumed to ashes – the people gazing with horror and astonishment on the sacrilegious act expecting that some signal vengeance would overtake the bold assailant of the gods. (Tyerman and Bennet 1841: 49)

Most accounts of this event have been based on the reconstructions of Ellis and the delegation. But if we return to the eyewitness accounts their emphasis is not upon a wholesale destruction of images. Rather, it is on the public breaking, by Pati'i, of a personal relationship with *his* god – probably not 'Oro – via a destruction of the god's image, and a transferring of his allegiance to Jehova by becoming a member of the *Bure Atua*.

Davies noted that there was talk among some of the Mo'orean leaders of banishing Pati'i but that they did not do so because he had the support of Pomare and 'had not med[d]led with theirs but only destroyed his own god' (Davies 1961: 184n2). Again, the reference is to only one god. This was a formal, public act of re-identification, an improvised act of rituopraxis performed in a way that only a head priest could have done.

And it was almost certainly not the first of such priestly performances. The LMS delegation was told that, appropriately enough, a precedent of a kind had been set by Pahi, the head priest of Taputapuatea temple and brother of the high chief of Ra'iatea. Pahi told them that when he was with Pomare at Tahiti, probably in 1814, he dreamed that a cat ripped open his face. Believing this to be the work of his god he 'baked' the wooden image with some breadfruit, thus defiling it, and ate the latter, perhaps devouring the god by association. The delegation added, 'Pomare, at the time, was very angry with Pahi for what he had done, but soon *afterwards imitated his example* and thus set one to his subjects which they failed not to follow' (Tyerman and Bennet 1841: 157, emphasis added).

There are no other references to Pomare himself burning a god-image. However, the LMS delegation did record a highly significant dinner conversation with Tati, a former head priest of Tahiti and the main source of Moerenhout's account of seasonal rites discussed in the last chapter: 'Tati informed us that when Pomare abjured heathenism he ordered him (Tati) to take an axe and chop his god to pieces' (ibid.: 163). This, Tati said he had done, in defiance of other priests.

The usual procedure for 'casting off' gods (*po'ara'a tu i te atua*) was not to burn them (although this was occasionally done) but to bury them in 'graves' three or four feet deep. These were dug in unfrequented places outside of the settlements and generally considered to be haunted (Henry 1928: 178, 208). Prior to the burial of the image, a priest recited the following spell on the *marae*:

> There is the casting off, I am casting thee off! Do not come in to possess me again; let me not be a seat for thee again! Let me not know ['*ite* = perceive] thee again; do not know me again. Go and seek some other medium [priest] for thyself in another home. Let it not be me, not at all! I am wearied of thee – I am terrified of thee! I am expelling thee. Go even to the Vai-tu-po (River in darkness) into the presence of Ta'aroa, the father of all gods. Return not again to me. Behold the family, they are stricken with sickness; thou art taking them, thou art a terrible man-devouring god! (Henry 1928: 178)

Handy notes that in times of sickness 'the sacrifice, as a substitute or scapegoat, received and took away the demon or spell of black magic causing the trouble' (1927: 193). In this case, the god-image itself became such a sacrifice. After the burial of the god-image a new one was made and consecrated at the next *pa'iatua* ceremony.

The performances of Pahi, Tati and Pati'i were improvisations upon this practice. The words spoken by Pati'i as he threw his image onto the fire may not have been those recorded above but the practice of addressing the god before it was returned to the darkness of *Po* and Ta'aroa appears to have been followed. The baking, chopping-up or burning of the god-image constituted a more aggressive act of separation from the god than its burial. The new element introduced here is the desecration of the god, the deliberate and defiant polluting of it as if it were a sacrificial victim.

Iconoclasm

While many Tahitian and Leeward Island priests had, by February 1815, already taken their lead from Pahi and Tati and possibly Pomare by joining the *Bure Atua* and destroying their personal god-images, no Mo'orean priest had yet done so. The great significance of Pati'i's performance was that it sent a message to his fellow priests and chiefs that the time was now right to shift their allegiance to Pomare and Jehova. It is possibly significant that he sent this message at a time of much sickness throughout Mo'orea, resulting in many deaths, including those of at least one local chief. The month after Pati'i's performance two missionaries returned from a tour of the island to report 'much sickness among the people, but much encouragement to preach to them' (Davies 1961: 184–85, 188).

In June 1815, at the beginning of the season of *matari'i-i-raro,* Pleiades below, and while his sister-in-law, Pomare-Vahine, was still in Tahiti, Pomare set out on a 'slow journey round Eimeo [Mo'orea] for the purpose of conversing with the people, to persuade the different raatiras [chiefs] not to persist obstinately in their idolatry but examine the bad foundation and evil tendency of their own system' (ibid.: 187). We have two reports of this journey, one written by Pomare himself during the tour and the other written by the missionaries some months later. Pomare wrote:

> This is an account of our journey – the Ratiras (or chiefs) are inclined to hear and obey the word of God … many there are that lay hold on the word of God. There are 34 or 36 [chiefs] in Atimaha [district] of this description. There are others of the common people that are left; they pay no attention to these things; but the Ratiras, they all regard the word of God. As for Maata [Ma'atea district], they all here, the Ratiras and common people, all of them have embraced the word of God – 96 new ones of this description. Not many of Haumi [district] have as yet regarded the word of god; but Hamuna has. Hamuna is a man of knowledge; he has been hitherto a priest of the evil spirit (i.e. an idol priest), he has cast away the customs of the evil spirit. I am *highly pleased* with these things … The idols of these Ratiras are committed to the fire, they are entirely destroyed … Should these Ratiras ask me to write down their names how ought I to act? Shall I write them? (Pomare to Missionaries, July 3, 1815, SSL; also in TMS IV: 275–76; original emphasis)

This letter was very much a progress report. Pomare's party was proceeding in an anti-clockwise direction from Papetoai in the north and they were now in the southernmost district of Ma'atea, intending to move on to the district of Haumi on the southeast coast. Ma'atea and Haumi belonged to a division of Mo'orea known as 'the upper flesh of the fish', this being one of the eight such divisions mentioned in the chant cited earlier (Henry 1928: 90–94). The priests and chiefs of Ma'atea, the district from which Pomare wrote, had entirely destroyed their god-images. Commoners had supported them, as probably signalled through their participation in a collective feast. No such collective agreement had been reached or signalled in Atimaha. The fact that Hamuna, a priest of Haumi district, had joined him but that others were yet to follow suggests the conversion through image destruction was a priest-led process. Pomare would certainly have been accompanied on his journey by Pati'i. Those who allied themselves with Pomare and Jehova became *Bure Atua* and hence Pomare expected them to want their names recorded on the mission register.

By the beginning of September, when the missionaries reported these and subsequent events to their directors in London, the Ma'atea iconoclasm had become generalized throughout Mo'orea (see Figure 2.4) and had spread to some districts of Tahiti. Their account was brief:

> Others followed his [Pati'i's] example both here and at Tahiti. Maraes were destroyed and the altars overthrown and the wood of them used to dress common food of which different classes and sexes partook at one common meal in direct violation of ancient prohibitions and customs. (Bicknell and missionaries to LMS, 5 Sept 1815, SSL)

By now, virtually all of the Mo'orean chiefs had joined Pomare and Leeward Islands chiefs under Jehova and were 'obstinate for going over to Tahiti in a hostile manner' (Davies 1961: 190).

In the wake of a military victory, it was accepted practice to plunder an enemy's settlements and destroy its temples, using the wood from its structures to fuel cooking fires (Henry 1928: 313; Ellis 1829b: 214). In this case, however, chiefs and priests deliberately defiled their own temples and, by association, themselves. In so doing they were breaking, in an absolute and permanent manner, their relationships with their gods before giving their allegiance to Jehova, and hence to Pomare. Because this relationship had been established and maintained through sacrifices (these rejected by *Bure Atua*), the use of

Figure 2.4. Rubble from an abandoned coastal *marae* on Mo'orea. Tahiti is in the background. Photo by Hugo Sissons.

sacrificial platforms (*fata*) as wood for cooking fires was a particularly emphatic statement of separation and re-identification. Having deliberately defiled their temples and themselves, the priests and chiefs were now free (*noa*) to eat with commoners and women. Like Pomare, who had refused to share his turtle with his gods – that is, to sacrifice it – the participants in the collective feasts ate their food without sacrifice to their gods. Instead, as *Bure Atua,* they would have been 'very particular in asking a blessing on their food' from Jehova (Davies 1961: 174).

Under normal circumstances, gods, who had been present during priestly performances and industrial enterprises directed by priests, were also present at the feasts which concluded the activity. Handy adds:

> In a sense, all religious feasts were sacramental in that food was believed to be shared between gods and men. On such occasions all members of the group, family, industrial or tribal, the living, the dead and the patron gods were welded together through the concrete bond of food shared. (1927: 196)

We can reasonably assume that after the sacrifice of local god-images, Jehova was accorded the status of 'honoured guest' at the collective feasts which concluded the events.

A new Mo'orean society, centralized through allegiances to Jehova and Pomare, was the ideal that Pomare and his priests sought to realize through their tour of the island; the priests and Pomare himself, as ultimate priest, actively mediated between Mo'orean society as a whole and Jehova as *atua* as they made their tour and initiated district meetings. Pomare insisted: 'this was my business in this journey; it was to make known to them the word of God' (see Pomare's letter quoted above). The exact details of the manner in which the god-images were destroyed were not recorded. It is most likely, however, that the priests of each of the main district temples burned the images, probably unwrapping them first as Pati'i had done. It is also possible that in some instances chiefs and priests presented their images to Pomare who had them burned. Whatever the case, priests and Pomare mediated a transformation of a wrapped *tapu* image into an unwrapped and desecrated one. The expected returns for these acts of allegiance to Jehova (via Pomare) were probably life, in the form of relief from the raging epidemic and success in the expected war with Oro's chiefs and priests in Tahiti. All of this occurred, as I have said, at the beginning of the chiefly season of *matari'i-i-raro*, when the *pa'iatua* rites should have been performed.

A Ra'iatean-centred priestly hierarchy had been put into play in the preparations for and final staging of the Mo'orean iconoclasm. The improvised performances of the priests, Pahi, Tati, Pati'i and perhaps Pomare himself, represented the rituopraxis of men with godly dispositions who were expected to take the lead in such matters of great cosmological significance. As Pomare's party moved around Mo'orea, district priests who were members of the island's priestly order and thus recognized the greater authority of Pati'i in cosmological matters must have felt pressured to emulate his performance on behalf of their districts. Pomare had probably gambled on their doing so.

Conclusion

In 1815, at the beginning of the season of Pleiades below and at about the same time as the *pa'iatua* rite was probably being performed by Pomare's rival in Tahiti, a negation of this rite was being staged across Mo'orea. Pomare and his allied priests and chiefs could not have sent a clearer message of their united opposition to Opufara and his allies. Rather than re-wrapping and re-consecrating their god-images, Pomare's priests publicly desecrated them. No feather exchange, through which an 'Oro-based hierarchy was normally reproduced, took place. Instead, it is likely that, as Farefau had done in Tahiti, the feathers were burned, perhaps in cooking fires. Certainly, the wooden temple structures suffered this fate. Rather than reproduce a strict hierarchical separation between chiefs and commoners, men and women, each normally participating in separate feasts during *pa'iatua,* hierarchical divisions were dissolved in collective feasts. Thus *communitas* replaced hierarchy.

This was the Mo'orean Iconoclasm, the initial episode in what I will term 'Pomare's Iconoclasm'. The wider event, which also took place in Tahiti, the Leeward Islands and the Austral Islands, is the subject of the next chapter.

3

Pomare's Iconoclasm as Seasonal Sacrifice

In his brilliantly quirky *Kings and Councillors,* Hocart argued for the ritual origins of all government and understood centralization to be a ritual process directed towards the securing of life:

> It may seem a roundabout way of centralizing government to let one god devour all the rest. It seems roundabout only to those who are still possessed by the idea that the primary function of the king is to govern, to be the head of the administration. We shall see that he is nothing of the kind. He is the repository of the gods, that is, of the life of the group. (Hocart 1970: 98–99)

Hocart further recognized that one of the ways in which centralization has been pursued is iconoclasm, noting that 'the struggle between idolaters and iconoclasts is at bottom a struggle between local autonomists and centralizers' (Hocart 1970: 248). In this chapter I seek to understand the destruction of images and temples throughout the Society Islands and Austral Islands, in broadly Hocartian terms, as sacrifices that initiated social transformations directed towards greater centralization. These sacrifices marked new beginnings and took place during the period of Pleiades above, normally a period of *communitas* during which old hierarchies were suspended in order to be later renewed.

Hocart understood sacrifice to be a 'cold-blooded pursuit of social welfare', central to which was an identification of the sacrificer with the victim. By identifying with the victim and *sharing that victim with the deity,* the worshipper 'became identified with the deity in order to exercise the same control over nature as the deity' (Hocart 1934: 502–3). The perspective on sacrifice that I develop here shares the Hocartian emphasis on the objective of securing life – as welfare, success in war, freedom from illness, protection from sorcery, and prosperity – but it also emphasizes that sacrifice has a distinctive temporal logic. Within anthropology, the temporal logic of sacrifice has been most usefully explored by Victor Turner, Valerio Valeri and Maurice Bloch. I begin, therefore, by considering their writings on the subject.

Sacrifice as Social Transformation

Turner, in his *Drums of Affliction,* introduced a view of sacrifice as 'symbolically constituting at once the end and the beginning of cycles of social development' (Turner 1968: 276). He went on to elaborate and generalize this temporal notion in a curiously neglected article on the reproductive and transformative dimensions of sacrifice (Turner 1977). The fact that blood is present in both birth and slaughter reinforces, Turner reasoned, the double character of sacrifice as exhibiting both regenerative and life-terminating aspects. Elaborating on the significance of this bloody symbolism, Turner wrote:

> Sacrifice transforms, like revolution in some modern doctrines, more violently and rapidly by an act of slaughter that both ends and begins. The hasty and extreme character of blood sacrifice may well be linked in simpler societies with social pressure for speedy and drastic action to resolve crisis. (1977: 202)

In what Turner describes as 'sacrifices of abandonment' personal and social renewal are brought about through the abandonment of social structure and entry into the domain of *communitas.* This movement is symbolically represented through sacrifice as a passage from death to life (1977: 213). Turner's answer to the puzzling question of why a ritual centred on death or decay should be understood to produce new life is that in sacrifice only the social-structural self is killed, enabling an 'anti-structural' power of renewal to be liberated: 'in "sacrifice of abandonment" power rooted in social structure is abandoned and offered while a second power is tapped to purify and simplify relations among group members' (Turner 1977: 214). There are two closely linked ideas in this argument: firstly, sacrifice is a temporalizing act – both an end and a beginning; and secondly, an aspect (usually hierarchical) of the social self is symbolically negated so that it may be reborn in *communitas.*

More recently, Lambek, echoing Turner (although apparently without recognizing it) has also noted that 'sacrifice is a negation of the act of giving birth and yet strangely like it' (2007: 31). Drawing inspiration from Sakalava rituals, he has argued that sacrifice is an 'exemplary form of beginning', one that cannot be undone, while at the same time it marks an ending, a departure and the 'death of alternatives not taken' (2007: 27). Unlike Turner, Lambek does not emphasize what is begun (for Turner, the transition from one collectively subjective state to another) but focuses instead on the phenomenological sharpness of the new beginning. He does recognize, however, that sacrifice may take the form of a conscious attempt to move out of conditions of conflict and social break-down and that in such circumstances people may engage in 'increasingly frantic attempts at establishing new beginnings' through sacrifice (2007: 34).

Valerio Valeri also makes no reference to Turner's 1977 article, nor, surprisingly, does he discuss any of Turner's writings on sacrifice in his book *Sacrifice and Kingship: Ritual and Society in Ancient Hawaii* (1985). Valeri shares with Turner, however, a focus on the subjectively transformative nature of sacrifice, a ritual that is, he claims, distinguished from others in that it involves the destruction of a living thing treated as an icon (1985: 67). Sacrifice, for Valeri, is a form of symbolic action focussed on the iconic offering that 'effects transformations of the relationship of the sacrificer, god and group by representing them in public' (1985: 70–71). With particular reference to a Hawaiian understanding of sacrifice, Valeri identifies three main stages in this transformative process. Firstly, there is a perception of a 'lack', which includes social disorder, disease and lack of personal well-being generally. Secondly, the offering (which is identified with the sacrificer) is destroyed and devoured by the god. Because the sacrificer is identified with the offering now encompassed by the god, the sacrificer has become, temporarily, a token of the god – Hocart's point. This stage of heightened conceptual focus on the cosmological order is followed by a final stage during which consciousness is re-focussed on a worldly human condition via a communal meal during which the offering is devoured by those participating in the ritual. Throughout this process, a transformation in the significance of the offering is paralleled by a transformation in the consciousness of the participants (Valeri 1985: 72–73). It is partly as a result of this transformation that sacrifices are deemed effective since a clearer, more ordered understanding of life comes to guide social actions (1985: 74).

This theory proposes an intellectualist and Durkheimian view of the phenomenological process identified by Turner and Lambek. It also shares with Durkheimian functionalism an under-appreciation of the fact that interests in maintaining the social order and developing a higher consciousness of its cosmological roots were those of priests and other elites in Hawai'i rather than commoners. Whereas for Hocart and Turner the transformation of the sacrifice through iconic destruction and collective consumption is generally life-enhancing, for Valeri it is consciousness-raising.

Bloch's contribution to the anthropological understanding of sacrifice has been to propose a thesis that is also strikingly similar to Turner's in certain respects, although, again, without reference to the 1977 article. Recalling Turner on the temporality of sacrifice, Bloch writes that 'in ritual representations instead of birth and growth leading to a successful existence it is a weakening and death which lead to a successful existence' (Bloch 1992: 4). In *Prey into Hunter: The Politics of Religious Experience,* Bloch proposed a general theory of sacrifice in which he speculated that, almost everywhere, it exhibits the minimal structure of sacrifice and collective reinvigoration (in his terms, 'violence' and 'rebounding violence'). Collective reinvigoration includes feasting that sometimes spills over into a heightened state of aggression.

The sequence of events that I am now about to describe generally affirms the temporal structure and socially-transformative significance of sacrifice highlighted by Turner, Valeri and Bloch. The destruction of god-images throughout the Society Islands and Austral Islands in 1815 and 1816 constituted 'at once the end and the beginning of cycles of social development'. This destruction was an abandonment of a divinely-produced and divinely-sanctioned social structure in order to bring about social renewal experienced as *communitas*. The iconic offerings were already icons, the god-images themselves. In all cases, feasts, during which men and women, chiefs and commoners ate together in collective defiance of hierarchy (*communitas* for Turner and rebounding violence for Bloch) followed the sacrificial destruction of god-images. All of this occurred during the season of Pleiades above, the beginning of which was usually announced with sacrifices.

The Tahitian Iconoclasm

By September 1815, the Moʻorean iconoclasm had spread throughout the whole island. The expected battle between Pomare's forces and those of his Tahitian rival, Opufara, took place a mere two months later. In response to an offer of peace from Opufara, Pomare and his now sizable Christian force returned to Tahiti in November 1815. They were holding their Sunday service in a recently constructed chapel near the 'Oro *marae*, Utuaimahurau, when Opufara's forces attacked (Newbury 1980: 40).

Joseph Barsden, an adventurer who had been brought up in the household of the New South Wales Governor, Philip King, has left us a remarkable eyewitness account of this battle. Barsden had landed at Moʻorea in November 1814 and had subsequently married the daughter of an Afareaitu chief, Omaumau (Rodwell and Ramsland 1999: 16–17, 25–30). He records in his journal (spelling and punctuation as in original):

> On the first day of November 1815, I joined the Kings party on an expedition against the Idolitrous Rebells of Tahiti. Pomare, at this period being determined to regain his long lost dominions in the Island of Tahiti, had a fleet acquipt of not less than 300 war canoes from the adjoining Islands of Emeo [Moʻorea], Huahine, Raiatea and Borabora. The principal Chiefs were Mahini [Mahine], Chief of Huahine, with Auna, Upapora, Hitote and Pomare Vahine, with all the other Chiefs and men of distinction who had lately embraced Christianity. (ibid.: 16)

Describing the battle itself, Barsden wrote:

[W]e hauled up our Canoes and remained unmolested until the morning of the 12th when our pickets gave the alarm that the Enemy was approaching in good order. We were all at prayers for it was Sunday in a large open shed which was about 150 feet long. When Prayer was ended we got the Canoes into the water and prepared for action, while our land forces took shelter behind a large Morai [*marae*] that extended to the waters edge. (ibid.: 35)

Barsden had been placed in charge of a six-pound cannon mounted on two canoes that had been lashed together. He reports that he fired his weapon into rocks above a group of musketeers and that the resulting rock-fall killed seven of them. Soon after this, the 'rebel' leader, Opufara, was killed by musket fire and the battle was effectively over. Pomare was, at this time, in a canoe about a mile off shore. He joined his forces after the death of Opufara. Barsden continues:

On the vanquished leaving the field he came in and landed near to were my Canoe lay and on landing he kneeled down and returned Thanks to the great Jehova for the victory. (ibid.: 36)

Ellis has written the fullest second-hand description of this episode, drawing upon an eyewitness account by his friend, Auna, one of the Huahine chiefs referred to by Barsden above, and upon conversations with other chiefs (Ellis 1834 II: 144–59). In addition, the missionaries briefly noted the event (Davies to LMS, 30 Mar 1816, SSL), Pomare himself also briefly described his actions soon after it and the LMS delegation led by Tyerman and Bennet recorded a brief version that differs from, but largely supports, that of Ellis. Most subsequent accounts, including that of Moerenhout, are based, more or less loosely, on Ellis's version. There are no substantial contradictions between these accounts and that of Barsden.

It had been normal practice after such battles for the victors to plunder the villages of the vanquished, killing those they found there and capturing chiefs who would become sacrificial victims (Henry 1928: 313). In this case, however, Pomare ordered his Christian forces to refrain from killing and instead sent a party of warriors to the temple of 'Oro at Tautira (see Figure 3.1). Their orders were to 'destroy the temple, altars and idols' (Ellis 1834 II: 152):

When the king despatched a select band to demolish the temple he said, 'Go not to the little island[s] where the women and children have been left for security; turn not aside to the villages or plantations; neither enter the houses nor destroy any property you may see; but go straight along the high road through all your late enemy's districts.' (ibid.: 153)

Figure 3.1. Tautira district, near the main 'Oro *marae*. Photo by Hugo Sissons.

Another version of Pomare's instructions, recorded by the visiting LMS delegation, has a greater ring of authenticity:

> The mountains are mine; follow not the vanquished thither; the *motus* (low coral islets where the enemy had left their wives and children) are mine; let them alone there also. Proceed only along the open ways. Take no lives; take nothing but the spoils which you find in the fields or on the roads. (Tyerman and Bennet 1841: 45)

Upon arriving at the Tautira temple, Pomare's warrior party met no resistance from the priests. The visiting LMS delegation recorded that some warriors fired their muskets into the *fare-ia-manaha*, where the images were housed, before entering – 'the house was afterwards pulled down when the wooden inhabitants were shot through and through and consumed to ashes' (ibid.: 163–64). In Ellis's version the wrapped body of 'Oro was brought out first and the warriors

> stripped him of his sacred coverings and highly valued ornaments, and threw his body contemptuously on the ground. It was a rude, uncarved log of *aito* wood, *casuarinas equisatifolia,* about six feet long. The altars were then broken down, the temples demolished and the sacred houses of the gods, together with their coverings, ornaments

and all their appendages of worship committed to the flames. The temples, altars and idols all round Tahiti were shortly after destroyed in the same way. The log of wood, called by the natives the body of 'Oro, into which they imagined the god at times entered, and through which his influence was exerted, Pomare's party bore away on their shoulders and on returning to camp, laid in triumph at their sovereign's feet. It was subsequently fixed up as a post in the king's kitchen and used in a most contemptuous manner by having baskets of food suspended from it; and finally it was riven up for fuel. (Ellis 1834 II: 56)

The 'Oro image, rather than enemy chiefs, would thus become Pomare's sacrificial victim, defiled as such victims always were, by being associated with food (see Figure 3.2).

Barsden, who visited the Tautira *marae* soon after its destruction, wrote:

[C]uriosity led me to this Temple at Tautira, the District of the Rebell chief Upufaro [Opufara] who was killed in the battle was called Papora [Papara]. The Temples, Godhouses and their ornaments and alters were all committed to the flames, the Idol was an uncouth log of hard wood hewn out of the Ito [aito] tree, or Brazellian fir. (ibid.: 37)

While the major temples, including that of 'Oro, were destroyed by Pomare's forces, it appears that most local settlement and district temples were destroyed by their owners in acts of allegiance to Pomare. Many people had

Figure 3.2. Human sacrifice on a Tahitian *marae*. Engraving by J. Webber. *Source:* Library of Congress.

taken refuge in the interior immediately after the battle, expecting retribution, but slowly they returned to their settlements to find them largely as they had left them. Ellis continues:

> The family and district temples and altars, as well as those that were national were demolished, the idols destroyed by the very individuals who had but recently been so zealous for their preservation and in a very short time there was not one professed idolater remaining. Messengers were sent by those who had hitherto been pagans to the king and chiefs requesting that some of their men might be sent to teach them to read and to instruct them concerning the true God and the order of his worship. (ibid.: 159)

There are no accounts that explicitly describe the feasting that must have immediately followed this Tahitian iconoclasm but we do know that after destroying their temples and god-images people considered themselves to be *Bure Atua,* people who prayed to Jehova and ate together in defiance of eating tabus (Williams 1839: 186–87).

In February 1816, soon after the iconoclasm, Pomare brought all the people of his district together for a feast, which he termed a 'prayer meeting': 'The Ratiras [*ra'atiras,* chiefs] and all the people of the district assembled leaving their houses without people' (Pomare to LMS, 19 Feb 1816, in QC I: 168). He then embarked on a tour of the island presumably doing likewise in each of the other districts.

Ra'iatea and Huahine

In addition to the military support from Mo'orean chiefs, Pomare's alliance with Tamatoa, high chief of Ra'iatea and the chiefs of Huahine and Borabora had played a crucial role in his securing power in Tahiti. Many of these Leeward Island chiefs had joined the *Bure Atua* at Papetoai in Mo'orea before the Tahitian and Mo'orean iconoclasms. The missionary, John Davies, records:

> And it is a fact that can be well substantiated that the congregation at Papetoai, the School and registered 'Bure Atua' was the nursery from which originated every church, not only in Eimeo [Mo'orea] and Tahiti, but also in each of the Leeward Islands. (1961: 305)

Pomare's Ra'iatean forces certainly considered themselves to be Christians: As they approached their home-shores in late November or early December 1816 a herald called out to a priest on shore that they were all *Bure Atua* and that they had brought no sacrifices: holding up some spelling books he cried, 'these are the victims – these are the trophies with which we have returned' (Williams 1839: 186–87; Davies 1961: 197). God-images would be exchanged for spelling books in Aitutaki five years later and it appears that an association between religious texts, god-images and sacrificial victims was being referenced here.

Like the Tahitian iconoclasm, those of the Leeward Islands would be improvisations upon the performances at Mo'orea, which in turn had been improvisations upon the first priestly performances, including that of Pahi, the 'Oro priest of Ra'iatea. The earliest published accounts of the Ra'iatean iconoclasm are by the LMS delegation, Tyerman and Bennet (1841: 144) and missionary John Williams (1839: 186–91). The LMS delegation's brief version is based on an account by Fa'ariti, formerly the leading 'Oro priest at Taha'a and a key participant in the events described. Williams does not name his sources but he moved to Ra'iatea 1818, three years or so after the events, and no doubt learned of them then. He and Lancelot Threlkeld provide additional details in letters to the LMS (Williams to LMS, 9 April 1821; Threlkeld and Williams to LMS, 8 July 1822, SSL).

At the time of the return of Tamatoa and his Christian supporters to Ra'iatea only about a third of the chiefs had adopted *Bure Atua* practices – and most of these had probably fought with Pomare in Tahiti. Influential priests continued to offer sacrifices on *marae* while sickness increased. Soon Tamatoa himself became extremely ill. Williams wrote:

> [I]t was proposed by one of the Christians to destroy Oro, the great national idol, and set fire to the marae, suggesting that perhaps Jehovah was angry with them for not having done this before. After a consultation upon the proposition, it was agreed that a party should go and carry it into effect. Summoning all their courage, these proceeded to the great marae at Opoa, took Oro from his seat, tore off his robes and set fire to the sacred house. (1839: 187)

Thus, as Williams tells it, Tamatoa emulated Pomare in the destruction of the Tahitian 'Oro. But in this case, the destruction is more clearly a sacrifice of 'Oro to Jehova in order that Tamatoa's health might be restored.

Fa'ariti, Priest of Taha'a, told the LMS delegation that upon hearing of this action he encouraged his high chief, Fenuapeho, to fight for their gods and heritage (Tyerman and Bennet 1841: 144). Threlkeld and Williams added that the priests of Taha'a brought sacrifices to Opoa and a priest, inspired by 'Oro, called:

> 'Give me men, give me men. I will go and wrestle with Jehova, I will drive him to the setting sun. Who is Jehova? Did not I bring him forth? Is he not a son of mine? I will destroy him. Come let us wrestle with him, his people shall all be banished, give me men, give me men.' (Threlkeld and Williams to LMS, 8 July 1822, SSL)

The 'men' that 'Oro required were, of course, sacrifices. Fenuapeho and the opposing priests and chiefs then sent a clear message to Tamatoa concerning his fate:

They erected a house which they encircled with the trunks of co-coa-nut [sic] trees, into which they resolved to thrust the Christians and then set it on fire and thus burn them alive. (Williams 1839: 187)

This was literally fighting fire with fire: the Christians would thus be sacrificed in the same way that their images had been destroyed. Tamatoa sought to negotiate a peaceful resolution, sending his favourite daughter to Fenuapeho to broker peace. This overture was rejected. As rain fell, a female priest of Oro's daughter, Toimata, sang:

Thickly, thickly falls the small rain from the skies;
'Tis the afflicted Toimata weeping for her sire [father].

Descriptions of the subsequent battle emphasize the smaller size of Tamatoa's forces, as in one orator's description of them as a 'little flock of kids' (Williams to LMS, 9 April 1821, SSL). However, Tamatoa's forces almost certainly had many more muskets and after a brief skirmish, Fenuapeho was taken prisoner. The priest from Taha'a said that his high chief offered his bare breast to Tamatoa's spear, but his life was spared. In 1820, the lands of Taha'a would be formally restored to him (ibid.).

Tamatoa and his Christian supporters followed up their victory by inviting Fenuapeho and the other captured prisoners to join them in a huge collective feast and so become *Bure Atua*. Williams wrote of the forced converts that 'few could swallow their food'. The initial sacrifice of 'Oro to Jehovah was now complete. The following day, all of the temples in Ra'iatea and Taha'a were demolished (Williams 1839: 190–91).

These events probably took place in late December or early January. Davies, stationed at Mo'orea, recorded in his journal on 10 January 1816 that a boat had just arrived from the Leeward Islands with the news that peace had been established. Notes written on paper and plantain leaves requested spelling books and teachers (Davies 1961: 197).

At Huahine, local chiefs and priests appear to have transferred their allegiance to Jehova at about the same time as Tamatoa's victory at Ra'iatea. We have two good accounts of the Huahine iconoclasm, one recorded by Ellis (1834 II: 253–54) and another by Tyerman and Bennet (1841: 75).

Ellis wrote that immediately after the Tahitian Iconoclasm, Mahine, the high chief of Huahine, sent a leading chief to the island to instruct his people to demolish their temples, burn their god-images and discontinue sacrifices. Presumably this message reached Huahine in November or December 1815. As the Ra'iateans had been, the people of Huahine were divided between

Bure Atua and those who wanted to maintain the old order. Thus, while the *Bure Atua* appear to have carried out Mahine's instructions, some chiefs and certain priests of the god Tane refused. As noted in Chapter 1, the *pa'iatua* rites at Huahine were centred on a large wooden image of Tane which was laid on a stone platform during the ceremony of Pleiades below. The decisive ritual conflict between Jehova's supporters and those who wished to retain allegiance to Tane appears to have taken place near this stone. Here is how it was described to the visiting LMS delegation by a chief or priest who had sided with Tane:

> Tane was brought down [from his house high on a pole] and laid upon that stone. The two bodies of warriors stood, face to face, so near together as to be ready to begin the battle. Hautia, one of our friends who is now with us, and Tiramano, the chief woman, were at the head of the Christians – for you must know that the chief women here buckle on the cartouch-box and bear musket before their troops as well as the chief men. When both sides were about to strike the first blow, Hautia and Tiramano made an offer of peace. They said 'you must soon fall into our hands or we must soon fall into yours; but if you will lay down your arms *now* we will be friends with you'. Then the true God caused the desire of peace to grow in our hearts and we answered 'we will have peace, we will not fight for those false gods anymore; we will submit to the true God'. And so it ended; peace was made between us; a fire was lighted just here; Tane's image was thrown into the flames and burnt to ashes before the eyes of both parties. Immediately afterwards, we consumed his house and destroyed his marae. We who had been rebels on account of our idols turned to the true God. And then a great feast was made and men and women ate together in proof that we had all embraced the gospel in our hearts. (Tyerman and Bennet 1841: 75)

The burning of Tane before the assembled forces was an improvised performance that recalls that of Pati'i. It was a public act in which the 'body' of Tane was sacrificed to Jehova, and as had happened during Pomare's subsequent circuit of Mo'orea, this ritual burning of the god was followed by collective feasting during which men, priests and chiefs removed the *tapu* that had been derived from their association with it.

Very little concerning the destruction of *marae* and images at Borabora and nearby Maupiti has been recorded. Ellis notes that 'the conduct of Tamatoa was followed by Mai and Te Faora, the Chiefs of Borabora and, finally in [Maupiti], the most remote of the Society Islands' (Ellis 1844: 222–23). Maupiti was under Mai's control at this time and *marae* were destroyed there at 'the end of 1816', probably November or December at the beginning of the period of Pleiades above (Davies 1961: 207; Tyerman and Bennet 1841: 150). In April 1817, the Mo'orean missionaries record in their journal:

> The people there [at Borabora and Maupiti], and particularly Te Paara, a chief of Borabora, are earnestly asking us to send them a teacher. The chief informs us [by letter] that the little island to the westward of them, Maurua [Maupiti], has also embraced Christianity. He went over there and by the conversation he had with the chief, his persuasions and the account he gave of the other islands, they resolved upon renouncing their idols and have consequently destroyed them throughout the islands, they have also demolished the morais [marae] and thrown down the alters so that now the whole of the group of islands have renounced heathenism. (Davies, Ellis, Crook, 21 April 1817, SSJ)

There were no missionaries in Tahiti or the Leeward Islands at this time: this was Pomare's iconoclasm, extended from Mo'orea and Tahiti to the Leeward Islands through the agency of his *Bure Atua* allies, principally Tamatoa, Mahine, Mai, Te Faora and Te Paara. In each of the islands this extension was a ritual process of seasonally appropriate social regeneration effected by the destruction of *marae*, the sacrificing of god-images and the staging of *tapu*-negating feasts through which a new *communitas* was produced. New Christian hierarchies would soon follow, and although tensions between the Leeward Islands chiefs and Pomare would increase, the Society Islands was now more politically centralized than it had ever been.

The Austral Islands

While King George III served as the royal embodiment of a foreign power for Pomare, Pomare himself served as the 'stranger-king' for social renewals in the Austral Islands. I conclude my account of Pomare's iconoclasm with a description of events in the islands of Ra'ivavae, Rurutu, Tubuai and Rimatara.

In early 1819, less than two years after Huahine's iconoclasm, Ra'ivavae was visited by a Huahine chief, Para, who had been a member of the *Bure Atua* at Mo'orea and attended school there. Upon his return to Tahiti in August 1819, his account of Ra'ivavae society encouraged Pomare, now flushed with his successes in Mo'orea and Tahiti, to extend his influence over this and other Austral Islands (Gunson 1966: 200). Pomare sailed with Para and an armed force to Ra'ivavae in October 1819 on an American ship exploring for sandalwood; Para had no doubt reported the existence of the trees on this island and that the island was divided by chronic warfare. Pomare kept a diary of this voyage. The entry for his second day on the island, 7 October, records that he gathered the chiefs together:

> I spoke to them: 'This is the word of God. Do not fight. Do not kill people. Do not steal. Do not lie. Do not pray to those evil spirits (varua 'ino) [god-images] in your keeping, give them up; do not keep them they are false! They listened to that, my words about their evil spirits to be banished. (translation in Gunson 1966: 202)

Pomare was able to negotiate peace and supplies of sandalwood, and he left Para on the island with guns and instructions to kill anyone who promoted a resumption of war. The chiefs of Ra'ivavae had passed the *hau* or 'supreme authority' of the island to Pomare and Para would serve as his representative.

Reporting on the visit later, the missionary Henry Nott wrote that people had 'with their own hands demolished their maraes before the King left the island' (Nott to LMS, 25 Oct 1819, SSL). However, if true, this does not appear to have been a general iconoclasm. This occurred the following year around the beginning of the season of Pleiades above. When Captain Samuel Henry visited the island in February 1821 he learned that the iconoclasm had taken place 'within the space of 4 months' which Ellis interpreted as meaning less than four months before his arrival, that is, in October or November, around the beginning of the season of Pleiades above. It happened, wrote the Captain, 'on a great feast day when all the natives and chiefs were assembled'. He found that a church had been built and the stone images from the temples had been converted into stools that stood at the entrance (Capt. Henry to LMS, 3 Feb 1821, SSL; Ellis 1832 III: 377). Defiling the bodies of chiefly victims after sacrifice was common practice throughout Polynesia and the transformation of the bodies of gods into seats, like the transformation of 'Oro into a pot-rack, was an improvisation upon this practice. The large feasts that accompanied the temple destruction probably included collective eating by men and women.

At the Austral island of Rurutu a devastating epidemic rather than warfare preceded ritual destruction. Here, by 1821, the population had been reduced from several thousand to only a few hundred. In a desperate attempt to escape death, a group of people sailed in two canoes to the neighbouring Austral island of Tubuai. Attempting to return home some months later, they were blown off course in a storm and spent some three weeks lost at sea. Eventually they landed at Maupiti and from there sailed to Ra'iatea where they joined classes in literacy and learned something of Christianity.

Au'ura, the brother of a chief who had died in the epidemic assumed a leading role among the group of survivors. He paid particular attention to the new religion, seeing it as a possible means to overcome the misfortune that had befallen his island. As he explained to John Williams: 'the vaerua ino

[gods] had been expelled from these islands – Tahiti Raiatea etc – and had gone there and killed almost all the chiefs and people' (Williams to LMS, 8 June 1821, SSL).

When Au'ura and his people were returned to their island in July 1821 they were accompanied by two Ra'iatean missionaries (termed 'teachers'), Mahamene and Puna. These missionaries described the subsequent desecration of god-images at Rurutu in a letter, dated 13 July 1821, sent with the images to the mission at Ra'iatea (Miss records XI: 277–79; Tyerman and Bennet 1841: 132–34). However, we need to treat this letter with caution. One missionary, John Jones, wrote:

> There has been some flourishing letter printed at the colony in reference to the conversion of the Rurutus or, as Capt. Cook called it, Ohitiroa, but the truth of some parts of it is doubted. (J. Jones to LMS, 6 April 1822, SSL)

Unfortunately Jones did not say which parts he doubted, nor did he give his grounds for doing so. The letter describes a meeting on 8 July of the 'King' and chiefs at which two priests opposed a proposal to abandon their gods in favour of Jehova. In response, a test of Jehova's powers was suggested by Puna, one of the Ra'iatean 'teachers':

> Prepare one place where you may all eat together, you, your wives and your children and your King at one eating place, and there the evil spirit [*varua 'ino*/god] who has now inspired that man shall be completely ashamed. (Tyerman and Bennet 1841: 134)

Threlkeld and Williams, to whom the letter was addressed, described the outcome as follows:

> They met accordingly and after satisfying their appetites without sustaining any injury they arose bodily, seized the gods, set fire to those houses, residences of their godships and then proceeded to demolish totally the maraes which was all completely effected that day. (Typescript with letter by Threlkeld and Williams to LMS, 8 Oct 1822, SSL)

It is extremely unlikely, given their knowledge of events elsewhere, that people would have expected to be immediately harmed – getting sick or dying on the spot. Indeed *tapu* would probably have been deliberately broken during the local equivalent of the Tahitian *matahiti* festivities. It is more likely that the feast signalled a collective intention to bring about religious change.

The images sent with the teachers' letter to the missionaries at Ra'iatea were displayed from the pulpit of the Opoa church (Williams 1839: 44–46). Among these was the anthropologically famous 'god', A'a, a magnificently carved container in the shape of a person with smaller god-figures clinging to the face and body (see Figure 3.3). Steven Hooper has made a convincing case that A'a was a reliquary in which the skull and long bones of a deified ancestor had been kept. He further notes that parallels might be drawn between it and Tahitian *fare-atua* (god-houses) in which wrapped *to'o* were kept – one being the transformation of the other (2007: 174).

There are no detailed accounts of temple or image desecration at the Austral islands of Tubuai and Rimatara. Pomare had landed briefly at Tubuai on his way to Ra'ivavae and had been formally recognized as the supreme ritual authority of this island also. As he would do at Ra'ivavae, he advised the chiefs to destroy their images and adopt Jehova as their God. The people of this island and Rimatara are said to have embarked upon general iconoclasms soon after, following the example of Rurutu (Davies 1961: 277, 284). The Tubuai iconoclasm appears to have happened the summer of 1821–1822, during the period of Pleiades above and a year after that of Ra'ivavae, because in the March 1822 they 'sent a deputation to Tahiti requesting teachers and books' (Ellis 1832 III: 385).

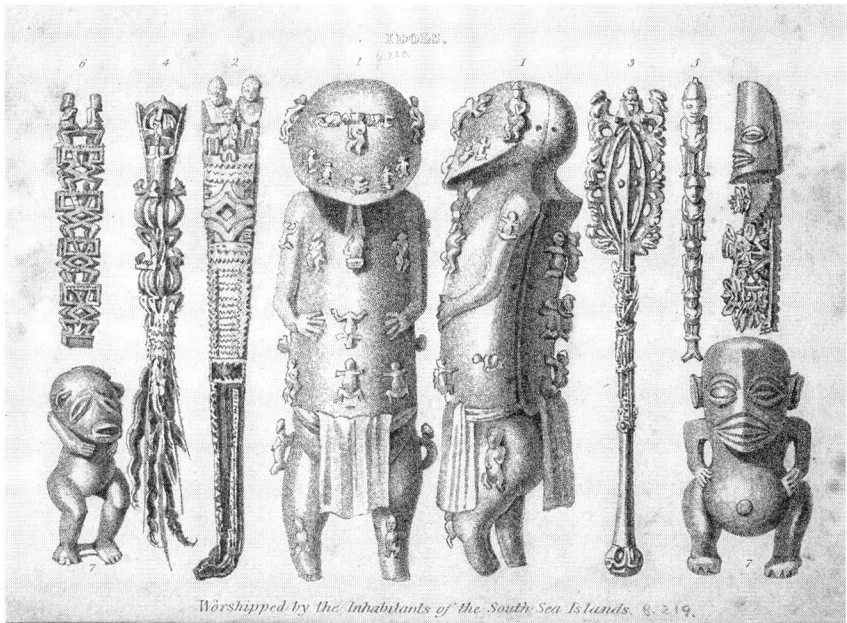

Figure 3.3. God-images from the Society Islands, Austral Islands and Southern Cook Islands. The large image in the centre pictured from two angles is named A'a. *Source:* Engraving from Ellis (1829b). Victoria University of Wellington.

Conclusion

The timing of Opufara's death in mid November 1815 was no accident. Missionary accounts make it clear that human sacrifice, feasting and armed conflict were usual at this time of year. As noted in Chapter 1, the missionaries recorded sacrifices on 17 November 1798. Some two weeks later, on 3 December, the missionaries learned that Hamanemane, the priest who performed the sacrifices, had himself been killed and offered as sacrifice at Taputapuatea *marae*.

In November of the following year, 1799, the missionaries wrote:

> Heard that in every district there is a small portion of land, the inhabitants of which are appropriated for human sacrifices. This morning a human sacrifice was brought into this district from Hapyano which they were taking to Pomare. Two of the brethren saw the corpse; it was tied up in a long basket made of cocoanut leaves; his head was much bruised with stones with which they killed him. It appears Pomare is sending to every district of the greater peninsular which is in his interest to send him a human sacrifice. By this it is manifest that something great is in agitation among them. (ibid.: 132)

Again, in November 1800, human sacrifices and rumours of war (ibid.: 135). In 1802, after a tour of Tahiti, the missionaries recorded widespread feasting and 'altars loaded upon offerings' and human sacrifices suspended from trees near the *marae* (ibid.: 154).

On Monday, 4 November 1805:

> Several of the King's servants are come over from Eimeo [Mo'orea]; they report that on Tuesday last a young man was killed there for a sacrifice and that several more are to be killed before the King comes over. (Missionary Society 1806 vol. 3: 169)

It was a similar story the following year (ibid.: 191).

In December 1808, when Pomare and the last of the missionaries hurriedly abandoned Tahiti in the face of overwhelming, island-wide opposition they left behind a calf and a picture of King George that had been given to Pomare. Both were immediately sacrificed to 'Oro by their enemies (Davies 1961: 130).

Opufara's priests had no doubt offered sacrifices before the final military engagement with Pomare's forces on 15 November. Sadly, Opufara, himself, became Pomare's first sacrificial victim in Tahiti; the wooden image of his god, 'Oro, was his second victim. The Tahitian Iconoclasm that followed was a collective improvisation upon a schema of sacrifice, orchestrated by Pomare and his priests at the seasonally appropriate time.

And as Hocart might have predicted, the outcome of the iconoclastic struggles described in this chapter was greater centralization. We will follow the unfolding of this aftermath in Chapters 5, 6 and 7. Before doing so, however, we need to consider the Hawaiian and Cook Islands iconoclasms. While these iconoclasms were less directly linked to Mo'orea than those at Tahiti, the Leeward Islands and the Austral Islands, both were carried out in the knowledge of Pomare's recent iconoclasm and, in the case of the Cook Islands, emulations were directly inspired by Ra'iatean missionaries. These more distant emulations are the subject of the next chapter.

❧ 4
More Distant Emulations

Hawai'i

On the first of November 1819, at the beginning of the *makahiki* season and less than a month after Pomare's visit to Ra'ivavae, Hawai'i's newly installed king announced the end of the eating tabus. This, before any European missionary had arrived in Hawai'i (Sahlins 1992: 57n1). During a feast held in a large building, 'nearly a hundred feet long and thirty feet broad' and attended by chiefs and foreigners from ships, Liholiho sat and ate with women, calling on the other chiefs present to follow his example. Men and women then 'sat promiscuously and ate the same food' (Tyerman and Bennet 1841: 100; Ellis 1828: 112). Immediately afterwards, Hewahewa, the head priest, resigned his office, 'the king declaring that there should no longer be any priests or any worship rendered to the gods' (Ellis 1828: 112). Hewahewa set fire to his temple and by the end of the *makahiki* season temples across the whole of Hawai'i had been burned down, some by priests, some by commoners. Many god-images were initially hidden in caves; however, almost all of these were also burned in 1822. This was the Hawaiian iconoclasm, a seasonal event that heralded the renewal of Hawaiian society.

Scholarly explanations of this event have covered the entire epistemological range from materialist to idealist. Kroeber (1948) famously suggested that it was the result of 'cultural fatigue', the effort required to maintain the temple rites being no longer meaningfully justified. Historian Kuykendall, and more recently, anthropologist Linnekin stressed the leadership role of chiefly women. Indeed, iconoclasm did serve women's political and economic interests, strengthening in particular the position of Ka'ahumanu, the powerful widow of Kamehameha, the King and father of Liholiho (Kuykendall 1938: 67; Linnekin 1990: 70–71). Webb (1965) proposed that the abolition of the eating tabus was a necessary prelude to the formation of a more economically rational and centralized state. Christianity, which would later replace the earlier religion, was not, of course, any more rational than the earlier ritual order. However, the increased freedom of movement for male chiefs and an improved ability of men and women to socialize together with Europeans would no doubt have assisted the growth of commerce.

The growth of commerce featured strongly in a related explanation by Davenport. He argued that the Hawaiian elite's lavish purchases had put them in debt which needed to be paid for with sandalwood. This led to increasing demands being placed on the labour of commoners who, as a consequence, were unable to both cultivate enough food for their own needs and, at the same time, support the priesthood and chiefly hierarchy (Davenport 1969: 18):

> My position is that the abolition of *kapu* was also a deliberate political response to a political crisis. The crisis was caused by rapid expansion of political jurisdiction and an increase in external trade; it was aggravated by growing religious skepticism and a declining population. All of these, of course, were set in motion by social and economic intercourse with Europeans. (ibid.)

Adopting a more Bourdieusian position, Sahlins has argued that the categorical significance of *kapu* had changed for Hawaiian chiefs and commoners as a result of practical engagements with Europeans, so that by 1819, when chiefs finally abolished the eating and sacrificial system 'they found many ordinary people ready to join them. Many had been doing the like for decades' (Sahlins 1981: 56). Sahlins is no doubt right that new understandings of *kapu* preceded new ways of living and eating together but the timing and dramatic way in which the latter were inaugurated did not logically or inevitably follow from the changed understandings.

For Sahlins the process of cultural change was set in train by Cook's visit to Hawai'i in 1778: 'the tabus began to disintegrate in Cook's time', he writes (Sahlins 1981: 56). I want to emphasize, however, that Cook's visit was also a political event of great regional significance. Within twenty years, by the mid to late 1790s, Hawaiian chiefs, who had learned of Tahiti from Cook, were exchanging gifts with Pomare's father (Pomare I), aspiring paramount leader of Tahiti, and planning a chiefly marriage exchange with him. Ellis, who had been a missionary in the Society Islands for eight years before moving to Hawai'i in 1823, was understandably curious about such connections between the two kingdoms. He records that Liholiho was to marry one of Pomare I's daughters and that one of Kamehameha's daughters was to become Pomare I's wife (Ellis 1828: 79). Unfortunately for the alliance, Pomare I died in 1803 before Kamehameha could arrange for a ship. The proposed marriage exchange is significant for us here, however, because it supports a view that Hawaiian chiefs would have maintained a close interest in events in Tahiti. Thus, when Pomare's son, Pomare II, initiated the Tahitian iconoclasm in November 1815, accounts of the event would have been of chiefly concern and debate in Hawai'i.

Hawaiians had been visiting Tahiti from at least 1813; missionaries complained in this year that Hawaiians had taught Tahitians the techniques of liquor distillation (Davies to LMS, 10 Sept 1813). In 1818 Toketa, a Tahitian convert to Christianity, travelled to Hawai'i and joined the household of Kua-kini, the brother of Kamehameha's wife. He would undoubtedly have given a positive account of the recent Tahitian events which would have subsequently been widely discussed by members of the chiefly elite, including Kamehameha himself. Ellis simply notes that the King had 'heard what Pomare and the Ta-hitian chiefs had done in the Society Islands' (Ellis 1831 IV: 126–27; see also Sahlins 1992: 89n16; Sahlins and Barriere 1979: 20). Although he down-played the influence of the Tahitian events on the Hawaiian iconoclasm, Rev. Sheldon Dibble also recorded that Kamehameha was aware of them:

> Someone from those islands told Kamehameha that Pomare, the King, had teachers at his islands, that he had made a great change in his worship and was learning the palapala (to read and write). Kame-hameha replied, rather in a way of unbelief, 'why then has he not sent a palapala to me?' (Dibble 1843: 143)

Given Toketa's presence, Dibble's implied claim that Kamehameha did not believe the story told to him about the Tahitian events is not credible. And what of the views of Kamehameha's wife, Ka'ahumanu, and others of her family who would play crucial roles in the Hawaiian iconoclasm after Kamehame-ha's death? Dibble is silent on these.

Clearly, there had also been other debates concerning the recent political and religious events in the Society Islands. In a report of their visit to Hawai'i in 1822, the LMS delegation headed by the Reverend Tyerman and George Bennet noted that there had been many Hawaiians travelling abroad in com-mercial ships prior to 1819. They describe a debate between one such traveller, Joseph Banks (named after Cook's botanist) and a priest during which Banks is said to have exclaimed:

> In England and America there are no idols, no tabus, yet there is plenty of rain there and fine crops too. In Tahiti and Huahine they have broken the tabus and destroyed the idols and worship the God of the white men – yet rain falls there and the fruits grow as abundantly as ever. (Tyerman and Bennet 1841: 115)

While these words may not have been exactly those of Banks there is every reason to suppose that such conversations did indeed take place. In my view, the Hawaiian iconoclasm was carried out in at least partial emulation of the recent events in the Society Islands or, at the very least, in the knowledge of these events.

And, as we shall see, the Hawaiian events did generally recapitulate those in the Society Islands. In both places the kings signalled their refusal to main-tain a sacrificial relationship with gods by breaking food tabus and the kings' actions were crucially supported by head priests who signalled their allegiance through iconoclastic acts. In both places, efforts to generalize this chiefly separation from the gods to the wider population were opposed by chiefs and priests who wished to maintain the sacrificial system, and in both places generalized iconoclasms occurred after the defeat of this opposition.

Many of the early accounts of the Hawaiian iconoclasm mistakenly assumed that a total destruction of temples and images occurred immediately after the November feast described above (For example: Kuykendall 1938: 67–70; Ellis 1831 IV: 122–28; Kalakaua 1972 431–46; Tyerman and Bennet 1841: 100). However, two of the best and fullest accounts, those of Dibble (1843) and Samuel Kamakau (1961), treat this feast as no more than a formal signal of intent that was not immediately followed by a total iconoclasm. Both Dibble and Kamakau drew upon information systematically collected from knowledgeable informants in the 1830s and 1840s. In 1836, Dibble organized his students at the missionary seminary in Lahainaluna to collect historical information and he later made his own systematic enquiries. Kamakau was one of Dibble's original students and he later headed a Hawaiian historians association (Sahlins 1992: 5, 8). The Dibble and Kamakau histories are in very substantial agreement over the way the Hawaiian iconoclasm unfolded and the following account is based largely on them.

Kamehameha I died in May 1819 leaving joint control of his kingdom to his son Liholiho and his widow, Ka'ahumanu; Liholiho's cousin, Kekuaokalani, inherited control over the temples of the war-god, Ku. As was customary, both Liholiho and his cousin went into temporary isolation after the death of the King. Food tabus had been suspended, and their confinement was necessary in order that they avoid pollution. Normally, the tabus would have been reinstated at the end of the mourning period when a new ruler was proclaimed. However, Ka'ahumanu, her brothers and Liholiho's very sacred mother saw in the king's death an opportunity for change. As noted above, many of the chiefs, especially the females, were finding that the sacrificial system and the demands of the priests had become a serious barrier to trade with foreigners. Ka'ahumanu, a 'woman of business', later commented that she and other chiefly women 'had long been disgusted with the *ai tabu,* the custom of men and women eating separately; as well as the impositions of the priests' (Bishop 1827: 247).

When still in isolation, Liholiho and Kekuaokalani were told of these plans and while Liholiho was reluctantly prepared to go along with them his cousin could not. Liholiho rejoined Ka'ahumanu and his mother in late October and was formally proclaimed king; His mother signalled at this time that the food tabus would not be re-established by sharing food with Liholiho's younger brother. Dibble, but not Kamakau, wrote that Liholiho's immediate response was to begin a drinking binge, and in the midst of this he travestied the customary temple rites. Continuing in his state of drunkenness, he subsequently spent two days in a boat at sea during which time, according to Dibble, he violated food tabus by eating dog-meat with women (Kamakau wrote that he did this immediately after returning to shore). In addition, the new king was seen drinking rum with female chiefs and smoking with them from the same pipes. When news of these acts became known to the chiefs it was clear to them that Liholiho would not re-establish the tabus. Dibble wrote: 'Hogs and dogs were immediately baked, other provisions made ready and chiefs, male and female, and Liholiho among the rest, sat down and feasted together' (1843: 150).

This feast would later be described as the key event in the collapse of the '*kapu* system'. But like the refusal of Pomare to offer a turtle as sacrifice before baking and eating it, this was a symbolic public statement of chiefly intent. Here is Ellis's description based on information supplied to him in 1822 by John Young, an advisor to Kamehameha who had been living in Hawai'i for thirty-six years and who was present at the feast:

> Hevaheva [Hewahewa] the high priest, of his father's war-god [Ku], said no evil consequences would follow the discontinuance of the worship of the gods. Soon after this, the king made a feast to which many chiefs of different islands were invited. The guests assembled, as usual; the men in one place, the women in another. The food was cut up by Mr. Young, from whom, as well as from some of the chiefs, we have received this account, and when all were about to begin their meal the king ordered his attendants to carry some fowls and such prohibited food to the place where his wives and other females were assembled; he then went and, sitting down with them, began to eat and directed them to do the same. A shout of surprise burst from the multitude around; several other chiefs followed his example. The men and women ate promiscuously and ate the same food, which they called ai noa, general or common eating, in opposition to the former ai tabu, restricted or sacred eating. The ai tabu was one of the perpetual restrictions imposed by their idolatry on all ranks of the people, from birth until their death. This public violation of it manifested the king's intention to destroy the whole system, which very shortly after was accomplished by the priests Hevaheva resigning his office and the king declaring that there should no longer be any priests, or any worship rendered to the gods. (Ellis 1831 IV: 127)

Surprisingly, Kamakau did not describe the feast, emphasizing instead the collective response: 'The pork to be eaten free was taken to the country districts and given to commoners, both men and women, and free eating was introduced all over the group' (Kamakau 1961: 225). Orders were received in Honolulu on 6 November 1819 that men and women should eat together and that women should eat pork, a food formerly prohibited to them. Collective eating took place on 7 November and some temples were destroyed the same day (Kuykendall 1938: 68). Dibble also notes that collective eating between men and women became widespread at this time (1843: 152).

Although some temples had been destroyed, the completion of the Hawaiian iconoclasm was still some weeks away. Certainly, Hewahewa had sent a signal that the priesthood would be dissolved by burning his temple and god-images. A European eyewitness, W. D. Alexander, recalled: 'The high priest himself set the example of setting fire to the idols and sanctuaries and messengers were sent even as far as Kauai to proclaim the abolition of the tabus' (quoted in Handy 1931: 26–27). Here, Hewahewa was acting in a similar manner to that of Pati'i and other Society Islands priests before the Mo'orean iconoclasm. However, sending a signal was one thing and gaining general compliance to its call was quite another.

As already noted, Kekuaokalani had refused to participate in or endorse these changes, attracting disenfranchised priests and 'a large body of people' to his cause. As happened in the Society Islands (and also, as we shall see, in the Southern Cook Islands) the outcome of this political division was military conflict, this one ending with the tragic deaths of Kekuaokalani and his wife. The engagement between the forces of Kekuaokalani and those of Liholiho took place in late December 1819 (Kuykendall 1938: 69). It ended soon after with the death of Kekuaokalani. He was shot in the left breast with a musket and 'immediately covering his face with his feather cloak, expired in the midst of his friends'. Soon after, his wife, Manoa, 'received a ball in her left temple, fell upon the lifeless body of her husband and instantly expired' (Ellis 1831 IV: 123).

After the defeat of Kekuaokalani, the iconoclasm that had been signalled by Hewahewa could begin in earnest. 'Immediately', wrote Dibble, 'the whole mass of the people made thorough work in demolishing the social inclosures [*sic*] and destroying their gods'. Of Kekuaokalani's supporters, he wrote:

> Their rage towards idols by which they had been so long enthralled and who had failed them in the day of battle was unbounded. They began the work of destruction. Some of their idols they cast into the sea, some they burnt and some they treated with contempt and used for fuel. They rushed to the temples and tore them to the ground. They slew Kaua, the priest who had exerted most influence with Kekuaokalani in leading him to uphold idolatry; they placed no restraint on their wrath, but vented it to the utmost acts of retaliation. ... It was not till after the war that people made anything like thorough work in casting off the shackles of idolatry. (1843: 157)

Thus was the Hawaiian Iconoclasm completed – according to Ellis (1828), the only god-images left standing were those at the royal mausoleum (see Fig-

The Depository of the Kings of Hawaii, adjoining the Place of Refuge at Honaunau.

Figure 4.1. Hawaiian kings' mausoleum with the only god-images left standing in 1823. *Source:* Engraving from Ellis (1828). Victoria University of Wellington.

ure 4.1). Occurring, as had the Tahitian iconoclasm, during the season of Pleiades above, the destruction was also associated with a period of generalized *communitas*: Alexander wrote that 'a general jubilee pervaded the islands, attended with revelry and license', a description that Handy aptly characterizes as a 'significant remark' (1931: 27).

The parallels with the Society Islands iconoclasm are not exact but they are close. As they had in the Society Islands, people expressed their allegiance to the new order and its leadership through destruction of temples and idols, in some cases using their wood to fuel cooking fires. The sacrificial victims were not only the gods in this case; they included a priest who had become a rival to Hewahewa. Dibble makes no explicit reference to the generalized feasting that took place after the destruction of the temples but I think it certain that pork and other offerings from the temples were consumed collectively by men and women during the 'general jubilee'. This had already occurred among the supporters of Liholiho and there is every reason to assume that it was now generalized throughout the country.

The final destruction of god-images was orchestrated by Kaʻahumanu at the beginning of the period of Pleiades below during a tour of the islands of Maui and Hawaiʻi. Auna, the Huahine chief who had fought with Pomare in Tahiti and who subsequently became a friend of William Ellis, visited Hawaiʻi with Ellis and the LMS delegation in 1822 and was invited to accompany Kaʻahumanu on her tour. On 4 June, Auna recorded in his diary:

Kaahumanu having commanded some of her people to go for the idol of Tamehameha [Kamehameha], namely Teraipahoa, it was brought today with nine smaller idols and they were all publicly burnt. (Extracts from the journal of Auna, SSL)

Other god images were presented to Ka'ahumanu at various points on her tour and these were stored on board ship to be taken back to Oahu. However, on the night of 23 June, a man who had been guarding the images became sick. The images were blamed and Ka'ahumanu ordered that they be brought ashore and burned. Eight named images were burned on the afternoon of 24 June. On 26 June Auna recorded:

Early this morning Kuakini's men who had been sent on board the ships for the gods returned. The chief [Kuakini, Ka'ahumanu's brother] then ordered his people to make a large fire and then set to work *himself* and with his people assisting him burnt one hundred and two idols. I thought of what I had witnessed at Tahiti and Moorea when the idols there were burnt at Papetoai by Pati and with my dear friend Jehova the true god that I had witnessed these people following our example. (ibid.)

Aitutaki

In the early 1820s Ra'iatea was beginning to regain its former priestly centrality. Evangelists from this island –some of them former priests – were sent not only to the Austral islands but also to the Southern Cook Islands of Aitutaki, Rarotonga and Mangaia. I conclude my narrative of the Polynesian iconoclasm by describing events that took place on the latter three islands.

The fullest account of the Aitutaki iconoclasm was written by John Williams, who said his description was based on an oral report from Papeiha, one of two single Ra'iatean men sent as missionaries to Aitutaki in October 1821 (Williams n.d.(a): 12–24, 43–55). Williams recorded that prior to the mission, the priests of Aitutaki knew of traditions that linked their island to Ra'iatea and at least one of their gods, Ruanuu, was believed to have originated there (ibid.: 53). The Ra'iateans had also told Williams of related traditions (Williams 1839: 104). The mission would thus be one of legendary and cosmological reconnection. The two Ra'iateans, Papeiha and Vahapata, were accompanied on their voyage by John Williams. Although the European did not go ashore, he did speak with a chief, Tamatoa, who came aboard the ship. Williams told Tamatoa of the iconoclastic events that had taken place in the Society Islands and 'other islands' (presumably Ra'ivavae and possibly Hawai'i) and urged him to follow their example (Williams n.d.(a): 12).

Papeiha and Vahapata were treated as powerful priests capable of sorcery by their counterparts in Aitutaki. Immediately after landing with Tamatoa, they were taken by two of his priests to his temple and they were subsequently expected to sit with these and other priests during a feast. They had arrived on 26 October, a week or so before the beginning of a festival of *pure ari'i* or 'prayers of the chiefs', this being the local equivalent to the *makahiki/matahiti* festival. The Ra'iateans were covered in great quantities of cloth, and thus concealed in the way that priests and chiefs normally were at this time (ibid.: 13). Indeed, we shall see that the whole sequence of events that would culminate in mass conversion in the summer of 1822 was closely tied to the seasonal ritual cycle.

As part of the 'prayers of the chiefs' festivities, different districts competed with each other in sporting and dancing festivals that were mainly held in specially constructed buildings termed *'are karioi*. However, sporting conflict could become more deadly military conflict and in the summer of 1821 it did so in a way that implicated the Ra'iateans. When one chief began his festivities before Tamatoa had completed his *'are karioi*, Tamatoa was angered and attacked the chief who had challenged his precedence. Tamatoa's forces prevailed on this occasion. Later, however, after Papeiha and Vahapata had taken up residence in the defeated district, these people gained a victory over Tamatoa, their presence then understood to have been the decisive factor in both victories (ibid.: 16).

After the summer festivities and conflicts through which, as Handy put it, the gods were 'exhilarated', sacrificial altars were progressively re-built throughout the island. Papeiha and Vahapata sought to undermine the integrity of this process. They received the tacit and then increasingly active support of the high chief, a fifteen-year-old youth who had begun reading and writing lessons with them soon after their arrival. During autumn rites known as *faatia-raa fata* or 'erecting the sacred platforms', the Ra'iateans publicly ate food offerings placed on these altars (ibid.: 19). Later, when altars 'of great size' were erected throughout Aitutaki, Tamatoa had one built close to the door of Papeiha and Vahapata's newly constructed house, thus treating the house as a temple. Perversely, however, the Ra'iateans also ate any food that was placed on this altar.

As Pomare had done on Mo'orea, the young high chief (also, confusingly, named Tamatoa) signalled his desire to abandon his gods in favour of Jehova by refusing to offer sacrifices to his gods. Indeed, on one occasion he broke down an altar and removed the offerings. No doubt influenced by what he had learned of the recent events in the Society Islands, the high-chief further emulated Pomare by publicly refusing to share his chiefly food with his gods, in this case shark rather than turtle. The food was cooked and eaten without a part of it first being presented on the *marae*. This act, like Pomare's refusal to sacrifice his turtle, appears to have occurred at the beginning of the season of Pleiades below. Moreover, it coincided with the high-chief's refusal to participate in what Williams refers to as 'the installation of the king', a ceremony 'of great pomp' – probably the *takurua* (ibid.: 44). In these actions, the high chief received the support of a local priest, Taita, who may have assumed a similar role to that of Pati'i and Tati in Mo'orea and Tahiti. Without the participation of the high chief, the rites of Pleiades below could not be successfully performed. As an expression of their grief at this situation, some women cried, cut themselves and smeared their resulting blood over their bodies.

Aitutaki now became divided between supporters of the high chief and those who sought to retain the existing system. Over the five-month period between the failed 'installation' and the beginning of the *pure ari'i* season of Pleiades above, popular support for the young Ariki and his new priests grew steadily. By December 1822 there was a 'general wish expressed to embrace Christianity': 'Whole districts, men, women and children with their respective chiefs at their head came and expressed their desire to be instructed and their determination to embrace Christianity' (ibid.: 46).

The arrival, a few weeks before, of a ship from Ra'iatea bringing gifts, spelling books and livestock (pigs and goats) no doubt contributed to the general shift in public opinion. So too, perhaps, did the destruction of a temple that had been ordered by the high-chief's grandfather: one of the grandfather's daughters had died after an illness, possibly brought by the ship, and the grandfather blamed the death on his own failure to join the Christians.

At an assembly of the whole island convened around the beginning of the *pure ari'i* season, the high chief's new priests, Papeiha and Vahapata, issued instructions that all temple structures be burned down and all of the island's god-images be brought to them so that they might be sent to Ra'iataea. The Aitutakian iconoclasm began the following day:

> The priests and chiefs of the different districts brought their idols and gave them to us and we, in return, divided our remaining stock of spelling-books among the several districts, which, however, only amounted to three or four for each district. All immediately began to work at the fare-bure-raa, or chapel. (ibid.: 47)

Feasts at which men and women sat and ate together took place a week or so later while people were at work building the island's first chapel. A turtle, normally food reserved for chiefs, was caught and the two Ra'iateans saw an opportunity to improvise a rite that would formally bring an end to the eating tabus:

> We sent invitations to many of our neighbours to come to our house with their wives. These were first all seated in a circle. All the old

prophets and priests dwelling near were then sent for and seated also. The oven was opened and the turtle brought and placed in the midst of the circle before they knew what they were sent for. We asked a blessing and then divided out portions of the turtle to women and priests and desired them all to eat heartily and without fear which they did. (ibid.: 47)

Rarotonga

In July 1823, Ra'iatean church leaders sent four additional Ra'iatean missionaries to the Southern Cook Islands – two were to serve at Aitutaki and two were intended for a new mission in Rarotonga, the exact location of which Williams had yet to determine. After landing new missionaries at Aitutaki and participating in a service in their new chapel, Williams set out in search of Rarotonga. He and the two prospective Rarotonga missionaries were now joined by Papeiha, Tamatoa (the Aitutaki district chief who he had met in 1821) and Tapaeru (a sister of Makea, a Rarotongan high chief). Tapaeru had been taken captive by a visiting ship at Rarotonga a few years before and left on Aitutaki.

After a week of unsuccessful searching for Rarotonga, the missionaries sailed for Mangaia where an attempt to establish a mission station almost resulted in the death of Papeiha. He had negotiated with a local chief for two missionaries and their wives to be allowed to reside on the island as teachers and had assumed an agreement had been reached. Accordingly, a boat was sent ashore carrying the new missionaries and their cargo, the latter including furniture, clothing and two pigs. Upon landing, the boat was immediately plundered, and there were attempts to strangle Papeiha with his poncho and rape the missionaries' wives (Williams 1839: 77–83).

The mission ship sailed immediately for the southern Cook Island of Atiu where it anchored off shore. A local chief, Rongomatane, sailed out to the ship on a large double-hulled canoe and was soon engaged in conversation with Tamatoa. The Aitutaki chief told the Atiu chief of the iconoclastic events that had occurred on his island and, by way of proof, showed him the offered-up god-images stored in the ship's hold. An 'astonished' Rongomatane spent the night discussing with Tamatoa and the Ra'iateans the dramatic changes occurring in the region and the following day he told them that he intended to follow their example (Williams 1839: 84–86).

Rongomatane had recently conquered the neighbouring islands of Mitiaro and Ma'uke and so he agreed to sail with Williams to these places in order to pass on what he had learned, inform the chiefs of his intentions and direct them to do likewise. Pleiades had just dipped below the evening horizon and the people of Mitiaro were preparing for the *takurua* rites through which Rongomatane would be installed as *ariki* for the island. The Atiu chief told them he would attend the *takurua* but only to monitor their steadfastness in constructing a new church. He then sailed with the missionaries to Ma'uke where, according to Williams, an identical arrangement was made (ibid.: 88–89).

Although the missionaries did not witness the resulting iconoclasms, reports from later visitors confirm that they took place (ibid.: 91–96; Siikala 1991: 117–19; Tyerman and Bennet 1841: 178).

Rongomatane was able to direct Williams to Rarotonga and this island was finally sighted on 25 July. After landing at Rarotonga, Tamatoa and Tapaeru informed the district high-chief, Makea, of the iconoclasm in Aitutaki and the Society Islands and said that they wished to leave missionaries with him to teach the new religion. Williams's plans changed dramatically, however, after Makea, exercising what he likely believed to be a chiefly prerogative, attempted to have sexual intercourse with the wife of one of the intended missionaries. As a consequence, the two Ra'iatean couples refused to remain at Rarotonga and Papeiha (see Figure 4.2) was left there alone under the partial protection of Makea.

Papeiha wrote of subsequent events in a letter sent to Williams at Ra'iatea in 1824 (Williams n.d.(b)) and Williams wrote an expanded version after he had spoken with Papeiha in 1827 (1839: 171–80). These, together with an

Figure 4.2. Papeiha and his son, Isaiah. *Source:* Illustration from Gill (1856). Victoria University of Wellington.

account later written by Maretu, a local participant in the iconoclasm, are our main sources.

By November 1823, Papeiha had gathered around him a group similar to the Mo'orean *Bure Atua*, this comprising mainly chiefly students, including the eldest son of Makea. In December, Papeiha was joined by another Ra'iatean evangelist named Tiberio. Shortly after Tiberio's arrival, the two missionaries set out on a tour of the island addressing the leaders of each district in turn. This tour, timed to coincide with the beginning of the Rarotongan season of Pleiades above, appears to have been a success. A few days after Papeiha and Tiberio's return to Avarua, a priest brought his eldest son to be taught, offering to destroy, in return, one of his wooden staff-gods. Papeiha accepted the deal. The image was duly unwrapped, cut up as if it were an animal and burned to ashes. As his improvised finale, Papeiha baked some bananas in the ashes and ate them (Williams 1839: 177). Paralleling events at Mo'orea and other islands, then, the beginning of the Rarotongan iconoclasm was signalled by the actions of a priest publicly destroying his god-image. Williams wrote that within ten days of this event 'not fewer than fourteen idols were destroyed'. However, fourteen wrapped idols were later shown to the missionary, Robert Bourne in 1825 and to Williams in 1827, which suggests that either fourteen new idols were later made or that these had been hidden by priests (see Figure 4.4).

'Immediately afterwards', wrote Williams, Tinomana, a high chief (*ariki*) from the recently conquered district of Arorangi, called for the Ra'iateans to destroy his *marae*. Papeiha's account was translated by Williams as follows:

> We all went to the marae which was soon destroyed by the flames; the evil spirit (they said) had fled to another marae called Mouaroa. In the morning we all assembled in order to destroy this marae in which the god had taken up his residence; this was demolished; they then said he had flown to another called Vaerota from whence also he was driven by the flames. We beheld the power of God in conquering Satan and praised him for the destruction of the maraes. When another day arrived we were fetched by another chief [Ariki of Takitumu district], Pa to go to the destruction of his maraes to which fire was put; they were soon in flames. (Williams n.d.(b): 293

Williams added that there was widespread shock at the actions of the high-chiefs and priests – women in mourning lacerated their arms and faces and smeared their bodies with blood as they had done in Aitutaki (1839: 179).

Papeiha wrote in his letter that Makea did not initially support the actions of the other two district high-chiefs and in fact tried to have the Ra'iataeans killed. In Maretu's eyewitness account of these events, however, Makea was the *first* to burn his *marae* and staff-gods:

The Makeas burnt their principal idols Pukea, Tangaroa, Manu-mao-mao, Eturere, Veteroa and Rangatira and the smaller idols. Their koutu [royal courts] Murivai, Araitetonga and Taputapuatea, and all the marae built by Tangiia (a founding ancestor) were also burnt together with all the other idols in Teauotonga [Makea's district]. Not one was left. Tinomana [head of Puiakura district] therefore burnt his idols ... three months after Rio's [Tiberio's] arrival on the island, Pa [see Figure 4.3] and Kainuku sent for Papeiha and Rio to come here to Ngatangiia [Takitumu district] and burn all their idols. (Maretu 1983: 60)

Irrespective of who was first, Maretu and Papeiha agree on the timing of the event. Maretu wrote that it ended in March, three months after Tiberio's arrival, and Williams appended a note to Papeiha's account above, in which he recorded:

[T]hey say that it was not till March 1824 that the destruction of Idolatry became general, then the conflagration of the maraes was general the idols all delivered up to the teachers and a large chapel commenced. (Williams to LMS, 2 Feb 1825, SSL)

On the Sunday immediately after this iconoclasm, a collective feast was held at Avarua in Makea's district. Preparations for the feast were begun on Thursday with a prayer meeting for the high chiefs and district chiefs (*mata'iapo*) at which they wore hats made from the wrappings torn off the destroyed images. On Friday, wrote Maretu, 'a message came for the people to gather food that day and cook it on Saturday. They would go to Avarua and could not cook food on Sunday' (1983: 62).

When Robert Bourne of the LMS visited Rarotonga in 1825 he estimated the population to be between 6,000 and 7,000. Of these, the Christians, most of whom were now living in Avarua, numbered between 3,500 and 4,000 (Bourne n.d.: 263–64; Maretu 1983: 63–67). This suggests that, while the people supporting the high chiefs were in a majority, a significant number – perhaps around 2,000 – were opposed to them and their new priests. These people retained their allegiance to opposing district chiefs and priests, refusing to destroy their temples and god-images. The missionary William Gill later wrote that seventy priests

vowed a vow over the sacred fires in their temple and, in the name of the gods, resolved to die rather than submit to the Gospel. These priests were aided and sustained by some of the great men of the land [*mata'iapo*] who did all they could to involve the two settlements in war. (Gill 1871: 15; see also Gill 1856: 34)

Te pa a Chief of Rarotonga

Figure 4.3. Pa Ariki of the Takitumu district of Rarotonga. *Source:* Illustration from Williams (1838). Victoria University of Wellington.

The destruction of these remaining temples and the capture of god-images became a preoccupation of the Christian leaders. A few months prior to Bourne's visit, Christian high-chiefs had demanded that non-Christian leaders pay them compensation comprising a god-image and a pig for blood that had been shed in a violent conflict between the two parties. When this was not forthcoming, Papeiha and Tiberio, the latter armed with his musket, led an attack on an inland settlement, plundering their property and capturing their god-images (Bourne n.d.: 262–63; Maretu 1983: 70–71).

Bourne was moved by the sight of the captured gods in 1825 and wrote: 'the cumbrous deities, fourteen in number (being 20 feet long and six in[ches] diameter) are now lying prostrate like Dagon of old before the ark' (Bourne n.d.: 262). The Biblical reference here is to the temple of Dagon where, according to 1 Samuel, the Philistines placed the captured ark of God. When the Philistines returned to the temple the following day they found that the statue of their main god had fallen over. Bourne appears to have left these deities in the safekeeping of the two new priests, Papeiha and Tiberio; as noted above, in 1827, they would be presented to John Williams and 'torn to pieces' in front of him (see Figure 4.4) (Williams 1839: 116).

" And the idols he shall utterly abolish."—Isaiah ii. 18.   (See page 30.)

Figure 4.4. Wrapped Rarotongan staff-gods being presented to Rev. John Williams in 1827. *Source:* Williams (1838). Victoria University of Wellington.

Mangaia

I conclude this narrative with Mangaia, the most southerly island in the Cook islands. While it is clear from the documentary sources that iconoclasms in Aitutaki, Atiu, Mitiaro Maʻuke and Rarotonga followed a seasonal logic tied to the appearance and disappearance of Pleiades, it is not possible to date the Mangaian iconoclasm with any precision. However, the decisive battle between Christians and non-Christians took place in February 1828, and so it is likely that the iconoclasm occurred in the summer of 1827–1828, some three years after the arrival of Raiatean missionaries.

In 1824, a year after Mangaians had driven Papeiha and his missionaries from their island, the Raʻiatean church made a second attempt to establish a mission station there. Two members of the church from Tahaʻa, named Davida and Tiere, were sent with the returning LMS delegation. This time the reception was more welcoming. An epidemic of dysentery had occurred immediately after the first engagement and it was thought that it had been caused by the Mangaian's ill-treatment of Jehova's representatives (Reilly 2003: 85).

Upon their arrival, Davida and Tiere were conducted by the leading inland priest, Numangatini, first to the main seaside temple, Orongo, and then to the main inland temple, ʻAkaʻoro, which was used for human sacrifices. A hut was built for the two foreign priests beside the inland temple (Gill 1894: 330). When Robert Bourne of the LMS visited Mangaia in October the following year, he learned that the two missionaries had moved to the leeward district of Keiʻa and established a Christian settlement they named 'God's Town'. They had built a new house for themselves, the cladding of which was 'whitewashed boards', and there was a small chapel nearby. Some of the inhabitants of three districts had joined them but the temples were still active and none of the leading chiefs or priests had abandoned sacrifices (Bourne n.d.: 259–60; Gill 1894: 330).

Sometime between this visit in October 1825 and February 1828, probably towards the end of 1827, members of the inland priest's family became ill. Siikala has rightly proposed that this was the 'final event motivating people to change their god' (1982: 149). Sickness and death had previously been interpreted to result from a rejection of foreign priests and their god, and if this new sickness was to be halted, the images of the island's main gods needed to be offered, as sacrifices, to Jehova's priest. Accordingly, all thirteen images were brought in procession from the inland temple to Davida's house at God's Town (Davida's companion, Tiere, had recently died). Gill continued:

> The day the idols were removed the house in which they had been kept [and fed] was set on fire; *maraes* all over the island were desecrated, the little houses in which the deity was supposed to be invisibly pres-

ent were burnt; the great stone idol of Rongo at the sea-side, where human sacrifices were offered, was smashed to atoms and (what is much to be regretted) the magnificent native mahogany (*tamanu*) trees were set on fire on account of their supposed connection with idolatry [the images had been made of this wood]. Coco-nuts were planted on the crest of the *marae* of Motoro [thus defiling a major god] in commemoration of this happy event. In their wild excitement the war-dance was actually performed as if they had gained an important victory! The heathen everywhere mourned the fate of their gods; but no chief was willing to do battle on their behalf. (1894: 331)

The war dance was possibly a case of Bloch's rebounding violence. We are not told whether collective eating occurred immediately afterwards but it probably did so. It had already become the usual practice for those living in God's Town, that is, among the Mangaian equivalent of the *Bure Atua*.

The actions of the inland priest, Numangatini, a member of the Ngati Tane tribe, were strongly resented by priests of the opposing tribe, Ngati Vara, and in February 1828 increasing tensions over the summer came to a head in the full-pitched and bloody 'battle of Poutoa'. Although Numangatini's supporters were less numerous, the opposition appears to have become divided so that the outcome was a Christian victory (Reilly 2003: 87). This battle of Poutoa was the final episode of the Polynesian Iconoclasm.

Conclusion

For Hocart, as I earlier noted, the whole life of a Fijian king was one course of ritual. So too was the life of Pomare and the other would-be kings who chose to ally themselves with him or emulate him, instigating their own iconoclasms in the Leeward Islands, Austral Islands, Hawai'i and the Southern Cook Islands. Through their actions, they, like Pomare, became the ritual centres for new, more centralized polities.

Pomare's iconoclasm, described in the last chapter, and those in Hawai'i and the Southern Cook Islands, described in this chapter, were connected episodes of a single regional event. What linked them were not simply the stories of previous happenings as told by Toketa, Papeiha and others, but also a shared seasonality of power that lent these stories credibility and political significance in Polynesian terms. Improvisations and emulations enacted as rituopraxis assumed the pre-existence of seasonally-orchestrated sacrifices, relaxations and re-impositions of food tabus, rites of hierarchy and its dissolution. While these were instigated by priests and chiefs, they also presupposed a concordance between their dispositions and those of ordinary people so that seasonality, although differently embodied, would continue to structure political life, even as revolution.

Mass participation in this seasonal revolution took on new forms in the aftermath of the iconoclasms, most notably as the provision of labour and materials for the construction of new churches, the subject of the next chapter.

5

Re-consecrating the World

Ua fenua te fenua
Ua marae te marae
Ua atua te atua
Ua ari'i te ari'i

The land is restored as land
The temples are restored as temples
The gods are restored as gods
The ari'i is restored as ari'i

The above lines are from the Tahitian *raumata-ohi,* a prayer chanted by a priest towards the end of a series of rites termed *raumata-vehi.* As noted in Chapter 2, it was common practice during the conflicts of Pleiades above to demolish the temple of an enemy and destroy or desecrate his god-images (Ellis 1829b: 214; Henry 1928: 313). The process of re-creating a divinely sanctioned hierarchy entailed rebuilding these temples, making and wrapping new god-images and purifying the land through the performance of the *raumata-vehi* rites.

William Ellis's description of this process is worth quoting in full:

> In addition to rites connected with actual war, there were two that followed its termination. The principal of these, Rau ma ta vehi raa, was designed to purify the land from the defilement occasioned by the incursions or devastations of an enemy who had perhaps ravaged the country, demolished the temples, destroyed or mutilated the idols, broken down the alters and used as fuel the unus, or curiously carved pieces of wood marking the sacred places of interment and emblematical of their tiis or spirits. Preparatory to this ceremony, the temples were rebuilt, new altars reared, new images, inspired or inhabited by the gods, placed in the maraes, and fresh unus erected. (1829b: 214)

The rites themselves began with prayers and sacrifices on the *marae.* Then:

> the parties repaired to the sea-beach where the chief priest offered a short prayer and the people dragged a small net of cocoa-nut leaves through a shallow part of the sea and usually detached small fragments of coral from the bottom which were brought to shore. These

were denominated fish and were delivered to the priest who conveyed them to the temple and deposited them on the altar, offering
at the same time an *ubu* or prayer to induce the gods to cleanse the
land from pollution that it might be pure as coral fresh from the sea.
(1829b: 214–15)

After the defeat of Opufara by Pomare's Christian force in November
1815, Opufara's close allies in Tahiti would, therefore, have expected their temples and god-images to have been desecrated and their settlements violently
plundered. They would have also expected that *raumata-vehi* rites would subsequently have been performed to re-consecrate the land and restore chiefly
hierarchy. Certainly, as we saw in the last chapter, the temples and god-images
were defiled. However, Pomare is said to have instructed his forces not to plunder the settlements. Many would have been the home settlements of Christian
Tahitians who had left Tahiti to join Pomare at Mo'orea and so this was not
necessarily as grand an act of Christian mercy as described by the missionaries.

More significantly, rather than performing the *raumata-vehi* rites and
restoring temples, the people of all districts of Tahiti and Mo'orea prayed to
Jehova and built chapels – over one hundred in total – and they held district
'prayer meetings'. Pomare wrote to the Missionaries at Mo'orea:

We have had our prayer meeting the beginning of the month, February. It was at Homai-au-vahi. The Ratiras [*ra'atiras*, chiefs] and all the
people of the district assembled leaving their houses without people.
They said to me 'write down our names'. I answered, 'It is agreed'. (Pomare to LMS, 19 Feb 1816, in QC I: 168)

It is not clear whether the district prayer meetings were held inside or outside. Pomare's may have been held inside a large *arioi* house of entertainment,
a few of which had been left standing after the conflagration that followed Opufara's defeat. Missionaries Davies and Hayward visited such a structure – 240
feet long and used as a church – in Pomare's Pare district during their tour of
the island in November 1816 (Davies and Hayward Tour, 25 Nov 1816, SSL).

John Davies wrote to the LMS in March 1816 to report that since the defeat of Opufara,

Pomare has been at Tahiti making arrangements about [the leadership
of] the different districts and overthrowing the vestiges of idolatry,
destroying the gods, maraes etc., the chiefs now zealously assisting
and erecting places of worship to the true god in every district around
the island. (Davies to LMS, March 1816, SSL)

The Tahitian churches were formally consecrated by Pomare during a tour
of the island in March (Pomare to LMS, 19 Feb 1816, in QC I: 167–69). On this

tour, Pomare probably also publicly approved and removed chiefly titles, 'careful to confirm in their divisional and district titles both friends and former opponents' (Newbury 2009: 149). Pomare expected that he would be asked to write down the names of chiefs on such occasions and this was a matter of some anxiety to him. During his tour of Moʻorea in June and July the previous year, he had written to the missionaries asking if he should record the names of the chiefs who had destroyed their *marae* and god-images and after recording names in February 1816 he asked, 'have I done wrong? Perhaps I have' (Pomare to LMS, 19 Feb 1816: 168, SSL). The name of a chief was *tapu* because it linked him with ancestry. The literary rite of recording names appears to have been understood as a swearing of allegiance to Jehova, via the pen of Pomare or that of a missionary priest. Pomare's concern may have been that because he was not baptized, and hence not a full member of the church, he was not the appropriate person to perform this solemn rite. He sought reassurance from the Missionaries again in 1816:

> When I go round Tahiti it may be that the Ratiras and others will ask me to put down their names, what shall I do then? Will it be proper for me to write down their names? (ibid.)

It could hardly have gone unrecognized by Tahitians that all of this was happening during the season of Pleiades above, a time for grand processions in all districts, a time for the people to seize the offerings made to the king, a time when the spirits of departed relatives returned with Roʻomatane. In 1816, Jesus Christ assumed the role of Roʻomatane. It was in his temples, rather than Rongo's houses of entertainment, that men and women collectively overturned *tapu* restrictions by worshipping together. There was some talk of replacing the *matahiti* festivities with Christmas celebrations. Pomare knew of these celebrations in Britain and at least two of the missionaries appear to have been in favour of this plan. But after lengthy deliberation, the missionaries decided against the idea. Prior to the iconoclasm, Pomare and his people had celebrated Christmas in *matahiti* style, that is, in a 'dissolute and shameful manner' and it would not be in the interests of the success of the mission to encourage such 'great profanity and wickedness' (Crook, 20 Dec 1816, SSJ). Instead, *pararaʻa matahiti* celebrations continued, until at least 1818, in combination with church services.

In November 1818, at the beginning of the season of *matariʻi-i-nia* marked by the rising of Pleiades, Crook recorded:

> The King began a tour around the island with a great number of people in his train … most of the numerous people that follow him acknowledge goods and property as their object, contributions [are made by] all the people of the two islands who bring vast quanti-

ties of food to the King, large rolls of cloth etc. These are distributed among his followers according to the old custom [of *parara'a mata-hiti*]. The people scramble for the property as soon as presented and leave nothing for the King himself. (Crook to LMS, Tahiti, 2 Nov 1818, SSL)

This was undoubtedly a *matahiti* rite as described in Chapter 1. Two years earlier, in November 1816, while they were making their own invited tour around Tahiti and opening chapels as they went, Davies and Hayward met an offshoot of the King's party proceeding in the opposite direction. This retinue was led by Pomare's wife, her daughter and her sister. Almost certainly, this was also a tour to receive and redistribute *matahiti* offerings (Davies and Hayward, 9 Nov 1816, SSL). A *matahiti* festival also appears to have taken place at Mo'orea some three weeks before. Crook recorded:

A great number of people were assembled whose behaviour was not very becoming or pleasing to me. I understand that a great quantity of food and cloth was to be presented to the chief … which in such cases is distributed among the people. (Crook, 16 October 1816, SSJ)

But as already noted, church services for Jesus Christ were also being held. As was appropriate for the season, congregations were splendidly dressed. At Mo'orea in November 1817, for example:

The greatest part of the congregation were dressed in beautiful white cloth, their heads anointed with sweet-scent oil, the females with their little cocoa-nut leaf bonnets and their heads decorated with red and white sweet-smelling flowers. (Williams to LMS, 16 Nov 1817, in QC I: 480)

The beginning of the *matari'i-i-nia* season continued to be celebrated, then, as a joyous time of feasting when the people seized the offerings of the king; only now a new god, Jesus Christ, presided over the festivities and their life-enhancing objective.

The church service in Mo'orea in November 1817 referred to above was probably held in a chapel built by Pomare. When in 1812 Pomare publicly abandoned 'Oro in favour of Jehova, he had also proposed, as we have already seen, that a substantial chapel be built for his new god (Davies 1961: 153). Missionary William Ellis wrote: At the same time that the King [Pomare] thus publicly desired to profess Christianity, he proposed to erect a large and substantial building for the worship of the true God (Ellis 1834 II: 95).

In the end, construction work was delayed (Davies 1961: 160), but the chapel was completed in July 1813 and enlarged the following year.

John Williams visited this church upon his arrival in Mo'orea at the beginning of the season of Pleiades above in November 1817. Here is his description of the building:

> There were some very good forms made of breadfruit tree, in colour something like mahogany. The building is made of round white sticks, placed about two inches apart and in shape resembles a hay-stack. The thatching which looks very neat is made of long narrow leaves and lasts about six years. The whole, including the doors, forms and desk had been done by the natives. We understand there are 65 of these chapels (some of which are very large) in the two islands of Otaheiti [Tahiti] and Eimeo [Mo'orea]. (Williams to LMS, 16 Nov 1817, in QC I: 478)

The 'round white sticks' were appropriate materials with which to construct the walls of this *tapu* building. They were probably the branches of the *purau* tree, the bark of which was used for making chiefly garments, especially *tiputa* (ponchos) and fine mats (Moerenhout 1983: 345). A similar chapel on the island of Taha'a, perhaps modelled on this, was described in 1822 as being built 'in an obsolete native style', having walls made from white *purau* stakes supporting a roof (Tyerman and Bennet 1841: 144).

The editor of the *Quarterly Chronicle* in which Williams's description of the church was published noted that there were, in fact, eighty-four such chapels at the end of 1816, not sixty-five. But they were both wrong, if the report by Davies and Hayward of their tour of Tahiti is correct. Their figures indicate that there were sixty-six chapels in Tahiti and a total of one hundred and two for both islands in November 1816 (Davies and Hayward to LMS, 1816, SSL). This large number – an average of one chapel for eighty people – strongly suggests that chapels had been built immediately after the iconoclasm to replace *marae* in all of the settlements. While Pomare's Mo'orean church may have been the model for some – certainly the Taha'a chapel appears to have been similar – they varied significantly in size, as had the former temples. Davies and Hayward recorded the dimensions of only eight of the sixty-six chapels. Almost all appear to have been narrow structures, between 20 and 25 feet wide, varying in length from 40 to 70 feet. The largest, built under the supervision of Tati, Opufara's brother and leading priest of Tahiti's Papara district, was 30 feet by 87 feet. Many of the buildings were without seating, suggesting that the congregations sat on grass matting as they would have done in the *arioi* houses of entertainment.

All the indications are that the chapels built in the immediate aftermath of the iconoclasm in Tahiti, Mo'orea and the Leeward Islands were in keeping with the seasonal spirit of *communitas*. They were certainly not the large, hierarchically-seated, centralizing buildings that would soon replace them. As

Ellis noted, the number of chapels in use 'greatly diminished' after 1818 as people moved to missions settlements (Ellis 1829b: 109). In Huahine, like Mo'orea, chapels had been built in each of the eight districts, each around 30 feet by 60 feet in dimensions, with a pulpit on one side. But after six of the districts relocated to the mission settlement at Fare in 1820 they were described as 'nearly all forsaken and decaying' (LMS report in QC II: 356).

Totalizing Temples: Hierarchy Restored

While the many small chapels that replaced *marae* throughout Tahiti in the summer of 1816 were formally consecrated the following summer during tours by Pomare and the missionaries, all but one of the large chiefly churches built subsequently were opened in May during the period of Pleiades below when *marae* had previously been restored and the *pa'iatua* rites performed. These large, socially totalizing temples, built in Mo'orea, Tahiti, Ra'iatea, Huahine and Borabora between the years 1818 and 1822, were massive projects of consecrated industry involving entire populations. In contributing labour and materials to these centrally-orchestrated projects, local chiefs and their communities signalled their collective recognition of the new hierarchy and their allegiance to its new god (Handy 1927: 172; Valeri 1985: 158). In constructing these new temples, the people were figuratively installing chiefs and affirming the new social and cosmological order that he embodied.

The term 'consecrated industry' is from Handy, who listed its main Polynesian features as follows:

> Organization and direction under master craftsmen or adepts and priests; worship of patron deities who were commonly deified men, by means of prayer and the presentation of offerings; *tapu* and purificatory rites designed to insulate the work, the workers and the product from evil; the taking of omens relative to the outcome of the enterprise; empowering workers, places, instruments and product by using conductors of *mana* and endowing them directly with *mana* through spells; consecrating the finished product by means of ritual; and finally, feasting and general merrymaking to mark the end of the consecrated period, to enjoy the product and render thanks to gods. (Handy 1927: 282)

It is difficult to tell from the available documentary sources to what extent the construction of churches was consecrated industry as defined by this list. However, it is likely that priestly experts (*tahu'a marae*) directed the early construction projects. Christian prayer services would have been held prior to and after the completion of chapels; and feasting everywhere concluded the projects. It is unlikely, however, that workers lived apart from their families during the construction of the larger buildings because, of course, the eating tabus had been abandoned.

The first of these large chapels to be completed was a renovated *fare potaa* – a long thatched house with rounded ends – rebuilt near the main *marae* at Moʻorea (Henry 1928: 93). The *fare potaa* was, according to Ellis, the most common form of chief's house, 'parallel along the sides and circular at the ends' (Ellis 1829a: 388). Such houses, when built for general meetings, might be up to 300 feet in length, with rows of large pillars down each side (Handy 1930: 19). Named Te Atae-pua, this large chapel had originally been used for *arioi* performances and large political meetings (Henry 1928: 93). A member of the visiting LMS delegation put it more colourfully: 'Here the doom of thousands, when hostilities were meditated, had often been decided by the auguries of the priests' (Tyerman and Bennet 1841: 33). He went on to describe the building as a long narrow structure, 210 feet by 45 feet, with 35 pillars on each side (ibid.). Pomare specifically requested that the missionaries attend the opening on 26 May 1818. They did so, preaching to a congregation of almost three thousand people, including most of the inhabitants of Moʻorea, the largest Christian gathering they had yet seen (Davies, 25–26 May 1818, SSJ).

Women were dressed in 'European fashion' for the occasion, appropriately so, because the main purpose of the gathering was to approve the constitution of a new Christian hierarchy, the Tahitian Auxiliary Missionary Society. Pomare became 'President', and 'Governors' (the term was used in the Tahitian text) were appointed for all districts in Tahiti and Moʻorea.

In April 1817, a year before this event, the missionaries had reported that work had begun on a large Christian temple for Pomare in his Pare district of Tahiti, a project that would involve the people of Moʻorea and Tahiti for almost two years (Davies, Crook, Ellis, 12 April 1817, SSJ; Missionary Records X: 251). Like the Moʻorean chapel, the idea for this building had 'originated entirely with the King and in its erection the missionaries took no part' (Ellis 1834 II: 380): 'The King, determined in his purpose, levied a requisition for materials and labour on the chiefs and people of Tahiti and Eimeo [Moʻorea] by whose combined efforts it was ultimately finished' (ibid.).

The missionaries were, in fact, opposed to so much time and property being devoted to it:

> But the King was not to be diverted from his original design ... He frequently observed that the heaviest labour and most spacious and enduring buildings ever erected were in connection with the worship of former deities, illustrating his remarks by allusion to the national marae at Atehuru, Tautira and other parts ... they ought to erect a much better place for the homage of Jehova. (ibid.: 381)

Pomare had failed in an attempt to ritually unite Tahiti through building a national temple in the Papara district in 1808, but ten years later he was determined to do so through the building of a temple to the new god (Henry 1928: 128, 138). Ellis thought it probable that Pomare also had 'some desire to emulate the conduct of Solomon … He enquired whether Solomon was not a good King and whether he did not erect a house for Jehova superior to every building in Judea or the surrounding countries' (Ellis 1834 II: 381).

The massive building might indeed have been seen as the Polynesian equivalent of Solomon's temple or, perhaps, one of the great Cathedrals of Europe. The most striking feature would undoubtedly have been its enormous length, 712 feet. A stream, about 6 feet wide, crossed at an angle towards one end, passing through special gratings in the walls. Thirty-six solid breadfruit pillars supported the ridge-pole and 280 smaller ones made up the wall posts, to which were attached planks of breadfruit tree, sanded smooth with coral. There were 133 windows with sliding shutters and 29 doors. The ends were rounded like those of the *fare potaa*, upon which it was loosely modelled. Some of the internal rafters were wrapped in sacred *purau* cloth, normally used for chiefly garments, and the ends of these wrappings hung down like banners from the upper part of the rafters. Other rafters were bound in coloured, braided sennit or coloured with dyes 'often presenting a chequered mixture of opposite colours, by no means unpleasing to the eye' (Ellis 1834 II: 376–77).

The opening or consecration of this temple took place in May 1819. As in the case of the new Mo'orean chapel, this was an occasion for a totalizing re-imposition of hierarchy. Pomare entered the building from the east, a direction associated with life, splendidly dressed in a white shirt, a chiefly waistband and a poncho decorated with red and yellow feathers. Already seated inside was Tahiti's entire population of 6,000 to 7,000 people, gathered around three pulpits more than 200 feet apart. From these pulpits, three sermons were preached simultaneously. From one of the pulpits at the eastern end of the building, Pomare then introduced a written code of laws and received their formal approval by the assembled masses.

Although this rite, like the *pa'iatua* ceremonies, took place as Pleiades sank below the horizon, it was in many respects dramatically different from the earlier Tahitian practice. While the *pa'iatua* had been performed and witnessed exclusively by male priests and chiefs, the new Christian ritual was an emphatically collective event – men and women, young and old, chiefs and commoners all sang and prayed together. At the same time, this event was an equally emphatic display of a priestly and high-chief-centred hierarchy. Pomare, dressed splendidly in chiefly garments, stood above the gathering of districts, each under the leadership of chiefs he had appointed. The building itself was a socially totalizing index of a restored hierarchy and was so closely associated with Pomare that after his death in 1822 repairs to it were discontinued. It soon decayed in sympathy with high chief's body, entombed nearby in a white-plastered house (LMS 1834: 191).

In 1816 and 1817, Ra'iatea and Huahine had, like Tahiti and Mo'orea, replaced their *marae* with small chapels in all districts. These were generally about 60 feet by 30 feet with pulpits on one side (LMS Report in QC II: 356). However, in 1819 and 1820, this time encouraged by missionaries, new centralizing settlements were built around large, socially-totalizing temples in both islands.

In Huahine, the population of six out of eight districts moved to Fare (see Figure 5.1), where the building of a new church was begun in early 1819 (Ellis 1834 II: 357–58). This and the Ra'iatean chapel were the first such Polynesian buildings to be plastered with a white cement made from coral (heated on a large fire to form lime powder) and sand. An association of whiteness with sacredness was thus materially extended from bark-cloth and *purau* stakes to coral cement. White cement was also subsequently used on the exterior and interior of many new houses, especially those of chiefs; the house of Tamatoa, the high-chief of Ra'iatea, was the first so plastered (ibid.: 343). A Huahine chief would later observe: 'We are thinking the word spoken by Jesus has been fulfilled … Tahiti is white, Mo'orea is white, Maioiti is white, Huahine is white, Ra'iatea, Taha'a and Borabora are all white' (Ellis and Barf to LMS, 23 Sept 1822, SSL).

Figure 5.1. Fare, Huahine in the mid 1820s. *Source:* Engraving from Ellis (1829a). Victoria University of Wellington.

The rafters of the Huahine church were wrapped in a similar manner to those of Pomare's temple in Tahiti. All districts had also contributed to its construction:

> According to ancient usage in the erection of public buildings, the work had been divided among the different chiefs of the islands: these had apportioned their respective allotments among their peasantry or dependants and thus each party had distinct portions of the wall, the roof and the floor. The numbers employed rendered these allotments but small, seldom more than three to six feet in length devolving on one or two families. This, when finished, they considered their own part of the chapel; and near the part of the wall they had built and the side of the roof they had thatched, they usually fitted up their sittings. The principal chiefs, however, fixed their seats near the pulpit. (Ellis 1834 II: 359)

This pulpit was hexagonal and was supported by six pillars, one for each of the districts that had joined the new settlement (LMS 1834: 177). The visiting LMS delegation was told, in 1822, that the island's two high-chiefs had each built a rounded end of the 100-foot long chapel and the middle had been built by their chiefs (Tyerman and Bennet 1841: 59–60). The seating was arranged around the hexagonal pulpit according to rank (ibid.: 51). Beyond the chiefly pews close to the pulpit, a wide variety of seating was evident, 'each family fitting up their own according to their inclination and ability'. Furthest from the pulpit were 'unappropriated sittings' – solid benches or forms without support for backs or arms (Ellis 1834 II: 360).

The temple was consecrated on 3 May 1820, at the beginning of the season of Pleiades below. The people of Ra'iatea (see Figure 5.2) had succeeded in completing their temple before the consecration of the one at Huahine, perhaps deliberately asserting their ritual centrality, and this was opened on 11 April 1820. Two thousand and four hundred people, again, the entire population of the island, assembled for the opening (ibid.: 361). This white plastered building, almost 200 feet long and with a courtroom on one end, also boasted chiefly seating around the pulpit. As had been the case in the church openings at Mo'orea and Tahiti, the consecration of the Ra'iatean temple was also an occasion for the re-imposition of hierarchy – in this case the formation of the Ra'iatean Missionary Society and the adoption of a written code of laws for the island (Missionary Society n.d.: 265; LMS delegation report in QC II: 427).

In 1822 – exceptionally, in February to enable it to be opened by the visiting LMS delegation – a new, large temple was opened in Borabora. All eight districts had contributed to its construction, a labour intensive project that took a year to complete:

Figure 5.2. Ra'iatea in the mid 1820s. *Source:* Engraving from Ellis (1829b). Victoria University of Wellington.

> The breadfruit timber was, for the most part, cut down in the mountains and dragged by man-force to the place where large boles were split in two pieces each making a separate plank and no more. (Tyerman and Bennet 1841: 86)

The whole population of Borabora, more than one thousand people, dressed in 'native garments' attended the opening and participated in the grand feasting that always concluded such events (ibid.: 84–86). This chapel was 70 feet long and had floors that sloped down from the sides towards the middle, thus enabling each side of the congregation to better see the other. Like the Ra'iatean chapel, this building also included a courtroom at one end, thus materially uniting church and state.

The last of the large Society Islands temples to be completed during the period 1818–1822 was an octagonal building that still stands (now fully restored) in Mo'orea (see Figure 5.3). This was opened in May 1822. The octagonal shape symbolized the island's eight districts and eight mountain radiations (Henry 1928: 89). Again, all districts contributed to its construction. It was built on the site of Pati'i's *marae,* which had been levelled to form the foundation, and stones from the *marae* were incorporated into its walls (Henry to LMS, 21 May 1822, SSL; Henry and Platt to LMS, 15 Aug 1822, SSL).

By 1822, then, the year of Pomare's death, a political field that included all of the Society Islands had been re-materialized in relationships between five

Figure 5.3. Octagonal church on Moʻorea. Originally built in 1823 and rebuilt, 1887–1891. Photo by Hugo Sissons.

new high-chiefly temples. Formerly such political fields had been materialized in relationships between the island's major *marae*, each of which had a genealogy that linked it with others and, in particular, with Taputapuatea at Raʻiatea. Pomare's 'Royal Mission Chapel' was by far the largest of the new temples. But the Leeward Islands chapels at Huahine, Raʻiatea and Borabora were just as totalizing, in that they encompassed whole societies or polities whose members were hierarchically seated within them.

Cook Islands Emulations

In 1822 and 1823, following the formation of the Raʻiatean Missionary Society, the new ritual field of the Society Islands was extended to the Austral and Southern Cook Islands. The Raʻiatean chapel, with its plastered walls and wrapped rafters, became the model for totalizing temples built in the aftermath of iconoclasm in Rurutu (Austral Islands) and Aitutaki (Southern Cook Islands) (Williams to LMS, 14 July 1822, SSL; Williams 1839: 61). A distinctive feature of the Rurutu chapel was the use of spears (minus their tips) to form railings around the table in front of the pulpit and on each side of stairs leading up to the pulpit (Ellis 1832 III: 401). They probably symbolized an intended peaceful hierarchy.

In the Southern Cook Islands, the Aitutaki church, while modelled loosely on that in Ra'iatea, was a more narrow structure – 180 to 200 feet by 30 feet – and it featured a white plastered pulpit (Williams 1839: 61). Building this chapel (possibly one of the buildings nearest the coast in the settlement shown in Figure 5.4) was, as it had been in the Society Islands, a collective enterprise involving the whole island, this work beginning immediately after the god-images had been presented to the evangelists of the Ra'iatean Missionary Society:

> The priests and chiefs of the different districts brought their idols and gave them to us, and we in return divided our remaining stock of spelling books among the several districts... all immediately began to work at the fare-bure-raa [sacred prayer-house], or chapel.
>
> Each district contributed posts – after the evangelists had instructed people on their preparation – and all participated in thatching and plastering. During the construction process men and women joined together to feast on turtle – previously a food strictly reserved for the ariki [high-chief]. This signalled the end of those tapu restrictions that had prohibited communal eating between men and women. (Williams n.d.(a): 47)

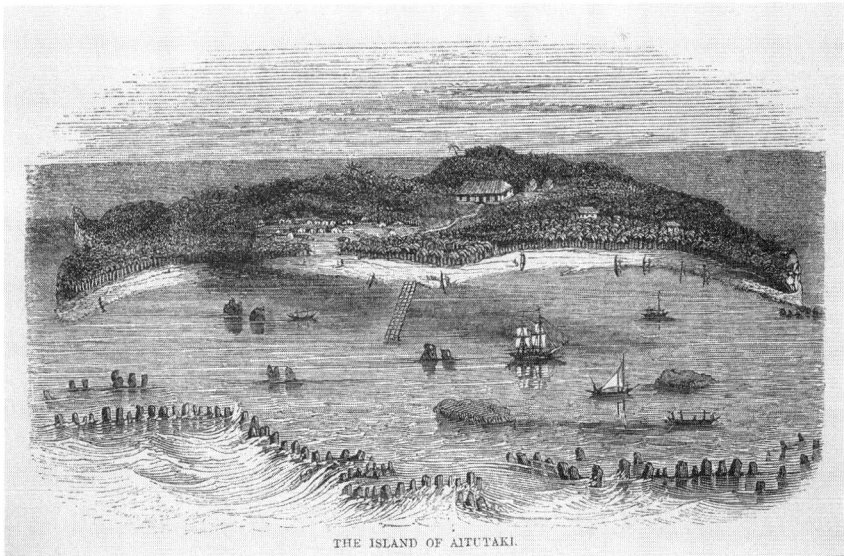

THE ISLAND OF AITUTAKI.

Figure 5.4. Aitutaki, Cook Islands, c. 1840, showing a large church (centre). *Source:* Gill (1856). Victoria University of Wellington.

In neighbouring Rarotonga, following the destruction of *marae* and images there in the summer of 1823–1824, the people became divided into supporters and opponents of the high-chiefs (*ariki*), leaders of the three districts, or literally 'canoes' (*vaka*). The *ariki* moved with their supporters – around two-thirds of the population – to Avarua, the present capital in the Te Au-o-Tonga district, where they formed a single, large settlement. Each sub-district of the three districts built itself a large dwelling and all the people began work on a very large temple, probably inspired by that of Pomare in Tahiti (Maretu 1983: 63–64 and n108). The building was incomplete when the LMS delegation visited in June 1824, but they were told that it would be 600 feet long. However, when Rarotonga was next visited in October 1825 a well-plastered chapel 240 feet by 42 feet was recorded instead (Bourne n.d.: 262). The missionary, William Gill, was later told that the two evangelists from the Ra'iatean Missionary Society – Papeihia and Tiberio – had preached simultaneously from two pulpits (Gill 1856: 28). John Williams, who visited the ruins of the temple in 1827, noted:

> One of the most striking peculiarities was the presence of many indelicate heathen figures [representing fertility and *mana* perhaps] carved on the centre posts. This was accounted for from the circumstances that, when built, a considerable part of the people were heathens; and as a portion of the work was allotted to each district unaccompanied by specific directions as to the precise manner of its performance, the builders thought that the figures with which they decorated their maraes [i.e., god-houses on marae] would be equally ornamental in the main pillars of a Christian sanctuary. The building was 250 feet in length and 40 feet wide. (Williams 1839: 124)

Tinomana, one of the district *ariki,* told Gill that the posts of the god-houses (*'are-atua*) on the *marae* had been 'the principal things of importance' and were always made from the best wood that needed to be without imperfection. These were carved, brought to the temples 'with great ceremony' and placed in wide, deep pits into which bark-cloth, axes and other offerings – sometimes human sacrifices – had been thrown (Gill 1846: 102).

We do not know whether any offerings were placed beneath the posts of the large Christian temple, but its construction clearly followed traditional precedent in other ways: it was a collective project animated by a sense of loyalty to district high-chiefs. Maretu recalled:

> The Makeas [i.e., family of the Avarua high-chief], Tinomana [high chief of Takitumu district] and their followers prepared a large feast of two hundred pigs and thirty bunches of pandanus. Thus the site of the church was cleared, timber for the ridge-poles and posts being contributed by each high chief and mata'iapo [sub-district chief] until

the whole building was provided for. And when all the ridge poles had been completed [the people of Takitumu district], under the chiefs, Pa and Kainuku and the mataʻiapo prepared a feast of seven hundred pigs and forty bunches of pandanus. Then the building was erected. (Maretu 1983: 64–65)

Maretu added that the work took a month. It was underway when the LMS delegation visited in June 1824 and so must have begun, appropriately, at the beginning of the season of Pleiades below when the rites of hierarchy known as *akaʻau takurua* were normally performed (Tyerman and Bennet 1841: 179). Completing the decorations took more than a month – the carved posts were wrapped with sennit or vines and the ridge thatch decorated with white shells – both consecrating actions (Maretu 1983: 65).

In 1827, the Christian population moved to the district of Takitumu where they again joined forces to build a second large chapel. This one, intended to serve only the district, was 150 feet in length. Bark-cloth wrappings from the abandoned staff-gods were used to cover the rafters of the building and some of the wooden images themselves were hung from these rafters (Pitman 1827: 16; Gill 1871: 14–15; Gill 1856: 32–33). Soon after the completion of this church, the triadic structure of Rarotongan society was re-asserted: Christian families left Takitumu to build new chapels and settlements in their home districts of Avarua (1828) and Arorangi (1830; see Figure 5.5). Three high-

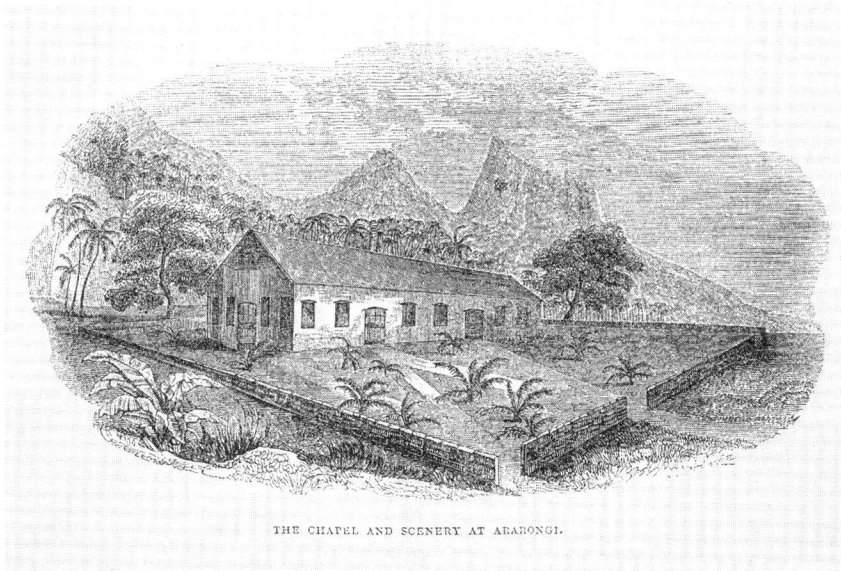

THE CHAPEL AND SCENERY AT ARARONGI.

Figure 5.5. The first Arorangi district church, Rarotonga. *Source:* Engraving from Williams (1838). Victoria University of Wellington.

chiefly district temples and their settlements were soon linked by a coastal road that encircled the island. This road, *the ara tapu* (sacred path), replaced the *ara metua* (ancient path), a path that had connected district *marae* and along which, as described in Chapter 1, annual processions of gods had taken place (Williams 1839: 207).

Chapels were also built in the other southern Cook Islands of Atiu, Maʻuke, Mitiaro and Mangaia immediately after the destruction of images and *marae* there. However, the documentary record tells us little about the processes of their construction (Williams 1839: 93–94, 241, 248–49; Tyerman and Bennet 1841: 178; Bourne n.d. 268; Griffin 1827: 213, 218).

Hawaiian Improvisations

In Hawaiʻi, where the iconoclasm of 1819 had not been directly mission-inspired (missionaries arrived the following year), the construction of grand chiefly residences initially assumed architectural priority over the building of churches. Chapels were built in two phases: initially, they were regarded as direct substitutes for chiefly temples, but after 1825 they became instruments of mass conversion and central to the creation of a puritanical Christian hegemony orchestrated by Kamehameha's widow Kaʻahumanu.

A decision to physically relocate the centre of royal power from Hawaiʻi Island to Honolulu was taken in September 1820, less than a year after the death, in battle, of Liholiho's main rival, Kekuaokalani (Bingham 1981: 132). Victory for Liholiho's forces was victory for a new political vision in which Europeanized royalty would govern, via sub-chiefs, a nation of peasants and serfs. In the wake of the iconoclasm, relocation of the king's household to Honolulu was an initial step in realizing this vision. Perhaps it was merely a royal whim, but Liholiho initially intended his palace to double as a church, an innovation that would surely have found favour with Pomare. The missionary Hiram Bingham, who discussed the king's building plans with him, wrote that immediately after the king's arrival in Honolulu in April 1821, Liholiho had agreed that the Christians could remain in Hawaiʻi and had requested their assistance 'in building a palace three stories high; the upper story of which, he said, should be devoted to the worship of Jehova' (ibid.).

The king must have had second thoughts about the practicality of this idea, however, and instead, he called upon the collective labour of commoners to build a large, single-roomed building, 50 feet long and 30 feet wide with a rounded roof, 30 feet high. To missionary eyes it had the appearance of a large Dutch barn, common at the time in United States. Inside, the pillars were 'beautifully hewn' and the furnishings rich, consisting,

... besides handsome mats with which the ground is everywhere covered, of three or four large chandeliers of cut glass suspended between pillars running through the centre of the building; of mahogany dining and pier tables; crimson Chinese sofas and chairs; several large pier glasses and mirrors; some tolerable engravings, principally of naval engagements and battles in Europe, likenesses of distinguished persons etc etc; and two full-length paintings of Rihoriho [Liholiho]. (Stewart 1970 [1830]: 101)

The palace was situated on the stone quay at the harbour 'under the guns and within a few rods of the wall of the fort' (Bingham 1981: 188). The full-length portraits mentioned in the quotation above no doubt conveyed a strong impression of Europeanized *mana* that was further symbolized in the furnishings.

However, like the *luakini* temples, the palace had been placed under a traditional *kapu*, the removal of which required payments from the subject population (Stewart 1970 [1830]: 101; Ellis 1831 IV: 418–19). All chiefs were required to display their loyalty by entering the palace and 'gifting' sums of money in sizes appropriate to their rank. Here is the remarkable scene as described by the missionary, Charles Stewart:

[Ka'ahumanu] was seated on a sofa at the middle of a long table covered with a superb cloth, having a writing desk open before her and a native secretary at each end of the table recording the names and taxes of the inhabitants of a district who were paying tribute. These were entering single file; and passing along the table on the opposite side of the Queen deposited their dollars before her and left the house at another door. Every twenty or thirty of them were preceded and followed by a couple of the King's body guard, armed with muskets and [in] a kind of uniform. (Stewart 1970 [1830]: 102)

Many chiefs presented between fifty and eighty dollars, and merchants and sea captains gave less. Over three days, several thousand dollars were collected (ibid.: 132). Ka'ahumanu, 'a woman of business', recorded the tributes in a roll-book in which 'the names, residence and tax of all the nation' were registered (ibid.: 102).

This *kapu*-lifting ceremony for the palace took place at the beginning of a two-week celebration commemorating Liholiho's coronation. This period, with its festivities and tax-collection practices was perhaps intended as a partial replacement for *makahiki* celebrations which had by now been abandoned. During the *makahiki* celebrations, taxes had been paid to priests of the god, Lono, as his image toured the islands (Campbell 1967 [1822]: 123). Replacing the processions of dressed images – a feature of the *makahiki* – was a glorious parade of extravagantly attired royalty through the streets of Honolulu. Ka'ahumanu was seated in a decorated whale boat carried on the heads and shoulders of seventy warriors, each of whom wore the traditional red and yellow feather cloak and helmet. Ka'ahumanu wore a scarlet dress and a crown of feathers and was shaded by an immense, richly decorated Chinese umbrella. She was accompanied in the boat by her cousin and the National Orator, both of whom wore silk loin-cloths and feather helmets. Two of Liholiho's wives were carried on double canoes while a third was a carried on a sofa. This latter was set ablaze in a dramatic reference to her name Pa'u-ahi (consumed by fire). The king's children were carried on a four-post bed. Like the *makahiki*, this was a time for *hula,* sexual freedom and revelry among the general population (Stewart 1970 [1830]: 116–20; Bingham 1981: 183–86).

In addition to the King's first palace, a number of other royal residences were built during the period 1823–1824 including, in 1824, a new and much grander second palace for the King. Ka'ahumanu had a house built for her use near the first palace in 1823, for which a *kapu*-lifting ceremony raised $800. This house and a second for her brother, Kuakini (also known as John Adams), governor of Hawai'i Island, were framed buildings purchased from the United States (Stewart 1970 [1830]: 132; Bingham 1981: 216; Broeze 1988: 100n6; Ellis 1831 IV: 419). The merchant Jacobus Boelen, who was invited to dine in Adams's home in 1828, described it as follows:

> The house where we were received was built of wood in the North American fashion. The whole frame had been transported from the continent to Kairooa [Kailua]. It included four rooms on the first floor, three on the ground floor, a kitchen etc. etc. (Broeze 1988: 35)

It was aptly described by Boelen as a 'princely home', surprisingly European in its furnishings and decoration (ibid.). The house was enclosed by a large stone wall, 10 to 12 feet high, the stones probably transported from one of the abandoned temples, confirming Sahlins's observation in passing that these 'civilized houses' were new temples (Sahlins 1992: 77). Ka'ahumanu's residence would have been similar to that of her bother in design and interior furnishings.

The earliest churches built by chiefs on the islands of Kaua'i, Hawai'i and Maui were built at a time when most of the population were unconverted to Christianity and unable to read. They were intended as chiefly temples intended to display chiefly *mana* and indeed they were 'known to Hawaiians as "*luakini*", the same term as that for royal temples whose construction was the privilege of rule in pre-Christian times' (Sahlins 1992: 71). Moreover they were built during the season of Pleiades below, at the time when such temples would normally have been erected, on or adjacent to the ruins of temples that had been destroyed.

The first of these churches was built at Kauaʻi by the chief, Kaumualiʻi, whose son had returned with the missionaries after a seventeen-year absence in the United States. It was built in August 1820 on the grounds of a destroyed temple and located near the chief's residence (Mykkanen 2003: 43). The first church on Hawaiʻi island was built by Kaʻahumanu's brother, Kuakini, in August 1823. Ellis, who was touring the island at the time, wrote that 'upwards of fifty persons were employed in carrying stones from an old *heiau* [temple] which they were pulling down to raise the ground and lay the foundation of a place of worship' (Ellis 1831 IV: 405). He added that the completed building was thatched and had walls 10 feet high. Kamakau tells us that this church was 'a great *luakini* named Mokuaikaua, the largest church in the islands. Outside, it was made of wattled *ti* stalks' (1961: 390). Soon after, similar churches were built in all but one of the districts of Hawaiʻi (ibid.). At about the same time, on the island of Maui, construction work was proceeding on a church for Liholiho's mother, Keopuolani (Mykannen 2003: 47).

King Liholiho and his wife died while on a visit to England in July 1824 and their bodies were returned to Hawaiʻi in May 1825. Immediately after the funeral, Kaʻahumanu and her siblings presented themselves for baptism and set about establishing a new Christian kingdom. In doing so, Sahlins argues, they followed traditional precedent by re-establishing the god, the sovereignty and the society simultaneously:

> [E]xcept the god was now Jehovah, she and her siblings were sovereign and the society was to be constituted by the tabus of Calvanist Christianity. In a way, the events of 1825, which saw the political imposition of Christian discipline on an indifferent or otherwise disposed populace, amounted to the sequitur to the overthrow of the old tabus in 1819 and thereby completed the mortuary rites of Kamehameha as well as Liholiho. (Sahlins 1992: 69)

The intention was to unify Hawaiʻi through a 'vast network' of churches and schools. The participation of commoners in church and school construction under the direction of chiefs was, like the cutting of sandalwood, compulsory – resistance was punished by burning down the culprit's house. Chiefs now had an equal interest in sandalwood gathering and church construction and the entire population of a district was engaged in one or the other activity at any one time (Sahlins 1992: 71; Mykannen 2003: 91).

In 1826, Kaʻahumanu, accompanied by her new missionary priests, began making circuits of the islands, consecrating or ordering the construction of new churches. The first of the Oahu circuits was initiated in July during the season of Pleiades below and Sahlins is surely right to compare them to the circuits made during the opening *luakini* temples:

In the same way as former paramounts (*ali'i nui*) annually made the circuit of the island after the festival of the new year (Makahiki) to re-open the local temples and thus reconfirm their reign, Ka'ahumanu and the several island governors made a habit of periodically circling the islands dedicating new Christian churches and announcing religious prohibitions. (Sahlins 1992: 71)

In 1829, the process of church construction reached a pinnacle with the building, under the auspices of Ka'ahumanu and the young King Liholiho II, of a very large church in Honolulu. It was consecrated, appropriately enough, on 3 July in a magnificent ceremony only rivalled by that of Pomare ten years before. Women had spread the entire floor with 12,300 square feet of matting and upon this some four thousand people sat to witness the event intended to advance Hawaiian nationhood. I conclude with Bingham's first-hand description of it:

> The King, in his Windsor uniform and his sister in a dress becoming her high rank and improved character and taste were seated on a sofa covered with crimson damask in front of the pulpit. Kaahumanu and other chiefs sat near. A little further in front of the pulpit sat the native choir of men and women singers, aided by a bass viol. The king had been made acquainted with the part which Solomon took in the dedication of the temple … When the congregation was ready, the king rose, and in a handsome, appropriate manner said in a few words, 'chiefs, teachers and commons hear: we have assembled here to dedicate to Jehovah, my God, this house of prayer which I have built for him. Here let us worship him, listen to the voice of his ministers and obey his word. (Bingham 1981: 344–45)

Like that of Pomare, this was the temple of Solomon re-built in Polynesia, a supreme effort in social re-totalization under the eye of Jehova. Within four years, however, the young king would contemplate pulling down Ka'ahumanu's temple. This and other resistances to new Christian orders will be discussed in Chapter 7. Before doing so we need to consider the significance of another form of material culture: texts.

🍀 6

Re-binding Societies

In December 1822, the people of Aitutaki in the Southern Cook Islands burned down the sacrificial platforms and wooden buildings on their *marae* within which god-images had been housed. The following day, these images were exchanged for spelling books in a grand ceremony that involved the entire population processing under the leadership of their district chiefs (Williams n.d.(a): 47; Williams 1839: 74–75). This ritual exchange dramatically re-enacted an equivalence between temple images and locally-printed missionary texts that had also previously been displayed in the neighbouring Society Islands and Austral Islands in the aftermath of generalized iconoclasms there.

In this chapter I pause the narrative of seasonality to reflect upon this association between god-images and books, with a view to understanding the ritual significance of Christian texts in the aftermath of the Polynesian Iconoclasm. Doing so, I also hope to contribute to an anthropological understanding of fetishism. Early anthropologists, notably Marcel Mauss, counselled against the use of the terms 'fetish' and 'fetishism' because they considered them to be too imprecise and to carry too much colonialist baggage. It appears that, in general, their advice has been followed (Ellen 1988: 214–15; Graeber 2005: 410). Roy Ellen made a useful attempt to reconcile religious, Freudian and Marxist understandings of the fetish within a cognitive model and Alfred Gell performed a valuable theoretical service in thoroughly blurring the distinctions between fetish, sorcery-doll and idol, rehabilitating the term 'idol' to refer to all such indexes of divine or semi-divine agency, irrespective of whether they are in human or non-human form (Gell 1998: 96–154). Most valuable, from my point of view, however, are David Graeber's more recent critical reflections on Pietz's historical account of the origins of the concept of the fetish in West Africa (Graeber 2005).

In this chapter I develop Graeber's insights into the creative nature of fetishism and demonstrate how, like sacrifice, it can be understood as a historically transformative phenomenon. My argument, briefly, is that in the aftermath of the Polynesian Iconoclasm, missionary texts were appropriated as power-filled objects through which new social relations were practically produced and morally bound. The extraordinarily strong demand for spelling-books across Eastern Polynesia between 1814 and 1824 and in Hawai'i after 1825 was due more to their ritual value in securing life than to the fact that they taught a technique for transmitting and storing information. A missionary printing press, established in Moʻorea in 1817, came to define a new sacred centre for the Society Islands from which fetish objects in the form of biblical texts and spelling books were distributed, these re-materializing a more centralized chiefly hierarchy. While I draw heavily upon the writings of Graeber and Gell in framing my discussion, I also owe an intellectual debt to Hocart, who not only wrote suggestively on the nature of idols and fetishes but who also connected them to social processes, notably centralization. In deference to age and wisdom let me begin, then, with his observations.

Fetishism as Social Creativity

For Hocart, there was no fundamental difference between idols in human form and aniconic fetishes such as carved sticks or clubs within which ancestral spirits were 'housed'. He wrote, for example:

> The human form is but one particular device among many and many peoples, such as the Fijians, do not think of it. They find their clubs quite as effective. (1934: 501)

Nor did he make a strong distinction between idols and totemic animals, noting that '[i]dols ... differ from relics and fetishes only in being fashioned after the likeness of a man or animals, from sacred animals only in being inanimate' (ibid.).

Instead, Hocart insisted that we should not lose sight of what all of these 'devices' have in common. All are material forms in which life has been 'fixed by consecration':

> The aim of all practical religions, those that count, is to bestow life upon matter so that it may benefit the community ... yet people quarrel about seeming inessentials such as the form of the vehicle, whether man or animal, image or aniconic symbol or complete absence of anything material. (1970: 245)

Hocart well knew, of course, that such quarrels are never really minor matters. In fact, they are usually serious disputes over who has the right to ritually control life and only secondarily about the means through which this project is pursued. He noted, for example, that in Fiji, fetishism was in direct conflict with colonial rule from London: 'The worship of numerous spirits housed in sticks or clubs and domiciled in Fiji was incompatible with the centralized rule of the Colonial Office' (1970: 248).

The problem was that the consecrated clubs housed alternative sources of power. Had all clubs represented the Governor (or housed his power) official concern would no doubt have centred on the distribution of the fetishes rather than their presence.

Graeber agrees with Hocart that we need not dwell on the distinction between idol and fetish. In Africa, 'idols' were first named by missionaries and 'fetishes' were first named by merchants, but both are humanly constructed forms in which spirits are believed to be housed. Appropriate, then, that Graeber begins his discussion of fetishism with houses and Marx's famous observation that, unlike the hives of bees, our dwellings exist first in the imagination. Graeber's point is that unlike houses, social orders are produced without plans – or at least they should be. It is in relation to this process of social creativity that we might best understand the nature of fetishes and fetishism. While Pietz sought to show that fetishes were originally misunderstood objects named in a West African context of intercultural misunderstanding, Graeber argues instead that they were 'revolutionary objects' through which radically new social relations were produced.

Tiv fetishes termed *akombo* participated, for example, in the creation of new markets. Consecrated when the blood from a sacrificial animal was poured over them, these images embodied and enforced peace agreements between rival lineages sharing the market space. Bakongo also used fetishes to create new social contracts, both parties driving nails into those frightening *minkisi* images in order to animate them. The key attribute of these objects and all objects that we term 'idols' or 'fetishes' is, according to Graeber, that from one perspective they are our own social creations while from another perspective they have power over us. We are, all of us, capable of viewing idols and fetishes from both points of view simultaneously. Any new social order or social relationship arising out fetish-making is

> an imaginary totality that could only come into real existence if everyone acted as if the fetish object actually did have subjective qualities. In the case of contracts this means: act as if it really will punish them for breaking the rules. (Graeber 2005: 430)

In West Africa, where new trading relations were being established between foreign and local merchants, the consecrations of fetishes were 'revolutionary moments. They involved the creation of something new' (Graeber 2005: 430). This is not to say, of course, that all fetishes are necessarily revolutionary, just that in certain historical circumstances their socially creative and morally binding properties render them so. Such circumstances include those in which Italian, Dutch, Portuguese and African merchants found themselves on the West African coast when trading for gold in the seventeenth and eighteenth centuries:

Merchants in West Africa who 'drank' or 'made fetish' together might not have been creating a vast market system, but the point was usually to create a small one: stipulating terms and rates of exchange, rules of credit and regimes of property that could be the basis of ongoing transactions. (Graeber 2005: 430)

Presumably, both local and foreign merchants acted as if the fetishes really had power over them, but if so, did they understand the agency of the fetish in the same way? This question of the agency of the fetish, left largely unexplored by Graeber, is taken up more directly by Alfred Gell in his book, *Art and Agency: Toward and Anthropological Theory*. Gell, like Hocart and Graeber, also refuses to make any firm distinction between idols and fetishes, emphasizing instead continuities between such objects as sorcery dolls, aniconic stones and god-images in human form housed in temples. What all these objects have in common is that they have been imparted with agency through particular strategies of animation. Gell usefully divides these into externalist and internalist strategies. The former strategies include the 'feeding' of idols and other manipulations by priests that impart a social identity. These, however, do not really impart a strong agency to the object (Gell 1998: 135). Of more interest to us here are the latter strategies which include placing substances inside fetish objects, wrapping such objects, placing them in containers and/or painting of eyes on them. In most cases these are not merely techniques for animating objects – they are practices of *consecration*. Indeed, confirming Hocart's view, animation and consecration amount to the same thing here.

With reference to a series of particularly striking examples from Polynesia, Egypt and India, Gell makes the argument that the consecration of fetishes or idols entails producing, reproducing or enhancing the illusion that they contain inner agency – 'homunculi' within bodies. This homunculus effect was most clearly demonstrated for Gell in the construction of the Rurutu god, A'a, a hollow human figure that was found to contain twenty-four smaller figures within it when it was opened by Ra'iatean missionaries. (Unfortunately for Gell, however, and as noted in Chapter 3, Hooper has cast serious doubt on the assumption that the gods found inside were normally resident there). Egyptian idols are described by Gell as having been housed in 'a box or ark which, in turn, was kept in the darkest and most central sanctuary of a vast temple complex' (Gell 1998: 136). This seclusion encouraged the attribution of agency on the basis of the equation, idol : temple :: mind : body. The Hindu idol Jagganath, a cylindrical section of a tree trunk, is consecrated when enormous eyes are painted on it and many Buddhist images are also imparted with internal agency through the painting of eyes on them by priests. Other interiorizing strategies described by Gell include the secretion of hollow stones (*mauri*) in holes in a forest by Maori priests and, most relevant to us, the wrapping of images with bark-cloth in eastern Polynesia and the construction of churches –

gigantic idols – within which the Christian God was 'trapped' (1998: 107–14). While Gell argues that in all these cases it is suggested that a 'mind' or 'mind-like' power is inserted into the object, I think this may be a too Indo-centric view. In Polynesia, it is ancestral power (*mana*) that is imparted to the object with consecration, power that is associated less with the mind than with ancestral presence more generally.

Let me now pull together the threads of the discussion so far into a more general understanding of the fetish as a socially creative and morally binding object. Following Hocart, we can minimally define fetishes (or idols) as consecrated objects that 'house' power. From Graeber I take the important idea that in consecrating such objects we imaginatively impart to them a moral power that is thought to act upon us to enforce or create new social relations. When these social relations form the beginnings of new social orders, fetishes may indeed become, as he says, revolutionary objects. Other fetishes, such as idols in human form housed in temples, while no longer revolutionary, continue to act in socially creative and morally binding ways. Hocart pointed to the importance of wrapping, pouring liquid over or painting eyes on fetishes as acts of consecration. Gell has taken this further, showing how a belief that these consecrated objects possess moral agency is fostered through practices that create the illusion of interiority. In sum, fetishes are consecrated objects that appear to have powerful interiors rendering them capable of creating and enforcing moral orders.

Hocart and Gell rightly stressed the very wide variety of objects that have been understood as fetishes – god-images in human form, sticks and stones, trees and animals. Given this great diversity it is not unreasonable to argue, as I am about to do, that in certain historical circumstances certain sacred books (within which the word of a god was bound) might also have assumed the role of fetishes. In what follows, I seek to demonstrate that immediately following the destruction of pre-Christian fetishes across eastern Polynesia in the early nineteenth century, spelling books and biblical texts served as substitute fetish objects through which a more centralized hierarchy was eventually enacted and enforced. It was not the case in nineteenth-century Fiji that the power of one governor was housed in many clubs; thus a centralized hierarchy required abolition of fetishes. In Eastern Polynesia, however, the power of one God, represented by missionaries and high-chiefs, was indeed housed in many books and thus a centralized hierarchy required their widespread distribution.

Fetishism as History

As noted in Chapter 2, the political history of Tahiti from the mid eighteenth century until 1811 had been centred on a struggle for ritual control over a wrapped and bound slab of wood, about the size a large man, but uncarved and without human features. This fetish (*to'o*), together with smaller versions kept at other *marae* housed the *mana* of the supreme god 'Oro, whose sphere of influence extended to the neighbouring island of Mo'orea and the Leeward Island of Ra'iatea where the main 'Oro *marae* was located. Ritual control over this fetish gave a leader control over life and death and the ritual distribution of *mana*, embodied in local fetishes, throughout the region. We have seen that the critical ritual, serving to both re-consecrate the fetish and distribute its *mana*, was the *pa'iatua* rite during which new feathers were exchanged for those that had been attached to images. The feathers, 'charged' at and distributed from a single source, participated in a ritual process of centralization as district and sub-district chiefs subsequently attached their 'Oro feathers to their own smaller fetishes kept at local temples. By offering and receiving feathers local chiefs participated with 'Oro's priests in the reconstruction of the 'Oro fetish, renewing the life and moral foundations of society.

After the destruction of *marae* in the Society Islands they were replaced by Christian temples. But in addition, a new ritual centre was established in Mo'orea: a printing press, set up at Afareaitu in June 1817, at the beginning of the period of Pleiades below. Pomare, whose authority was now more secure in Tahiti, had insisted in the strongest possible terms that the press should be sited near his residence there, but his new priests had been equally insistent that it should be established in the Leeward Island of Huahine. In March 1817 the LMS missionaries John Davies and William Ellis wrote in their journal that Pomare had objected in 'remarkably strong language' in letters sent to 'several individuals' to the plan to set up the press in the Leeward Islands rather than Tahiti. Others, probably local chiefs, told the missionaries that they were so upset by the proposals that they could not sleep at night. Faced with such opposition the missionaries had little choice but to compromise and set up Pomare's press at Mo'orea (Davies and Ellis, 1 March 1817, SSJ). If the press was to operate under the *mana* of Pomare, reflecting his ritual centrality in the transformed society, then it needed to be sited in close physical proximity to this high-chief who aspired to be 'king'. Later that year, the missionaries revisited the issue and re-affirmed their intentions to move the press to the Leeward Islands and this time it was Pomare who compromised – he intended to move with it. The missionaries feared that the removal of both press and Pomare as ritual centres would leave the windward islands of Tahiti and Mo'orea in a state of near chaos. Crook wrote in his journal:

> I dread the consequences of this [move] and fear the Windward Islands will be left in a state of anarchy and that all the best of the people will emigrate. Was the press to remain at these islands in all probability all would have been well. (Crook, 18 Aug 1817, SSJ)

When setting up the press at Moʻorea associations with the former rit-ual order were reinforced through the use of polished stones from the adja-cent, recently abandoned *marae* for the floor of the press-house. It had been normal practice to use stones from a pre-existing *marae* as corner-stones for new *marae,* thus materializing genealogical and political connections between them (Henry 1928: 132, 142). In using *marae* stones to form the floor of the press-house connections between old and new ritual centres were similarly asserted. Also boasting the island's first glass window, the press-house was de-scribed by one missionary as 'the finest building on the island' (Lingenfelter 1967: 6).

Further associations between *marae, paʻiatua* rites and the press were ev-ident in the ritual restrictions that surrounded the printing, by Pomare, of the first pages. As described by William Ellis, a trained printer who supervised the operation, Pomare carried out the operation in virtual secrecy:

> He came attended by only two of his favourite chiefs. They were, how-ever, followed by a numerous train of his attendants etc. who had by some means heard that the work was about to commence. Crowds of natives were already collected around the door but they made way for him and after he and his two companions had been admitted the door was closed and the small window next the sea darkened as he did not wish to be overlooked by the people outside. (Ellis 1829a: 393)

In Tonga, the building which housed the first mission press was consid-ered too sacred for commoners to enter (Daley 2008: 373). A similar attitude appears to have prevailed in Moʻorea. Appropriately, Ellis's main assistant at the press was Patiʻi, the former head priest of Moʻorea who had been the first to ceremonially destroy his god-images there in 1814.

As sacred centres often do, the press became a gathering point for large numbers of people seeking divine blessings. One missionary likened the whole district in which the press was located to a public fairground (Missionary Society n.d.: 240). The beach was lined with dozens of canoes from all over Moʻorea and Tahiti and hundreds of people erected temporary shelters around the press 'in every direction' in which to reside while waiting to receive their books (ibid.; see Figure 6.1). When a translation of the Gospel of Luke by Po-mare and Henry Nott was printed in November 1817 many people waited in such shelters for five or six weeks apprehensive that they might miss out on receiving a copy. Ellis described the actions of one group upon receiving their books as follows:

> Each wrapped his book up in a piece of white native cloth, put it in his bosom, wished me good morning and without, I believe, eating or drinking, or calling on any person in the settlement hastened to the

Figure 6.1. Site of the first Polynesian printing press, Moʻorea. Photo by Hugo Sissons.

beach, launched their canoe, hoisted their matting sail and steered, rejoicing to their native island. (Ellis 1829a: 405)

Thus, like sacred feathers, sacred words were distributed from a ritual centre to villages throughout Moʻorea and Tahiti. Both red feathers and printed words were indexes of divine *mana* centrally produced and associated with a single deity. Red feathers mythically originated with ʻOro in his bird form and had further absorbed his *mana* through being wrapped with, or attached to, the ʻOro fetish. Prior to the setting up of the press it was common practice to keep small pieces of paper on which scripture recited in church was written 'in a neat little basket'. These local 'amulets' were 'envied treasures' (Ellis 1832 III: 7). Higher status people constructed their own books or carried rolls of barkcloth on which scripture extracts had been neatly written:

The bark of the paper mulberry was frequently beaten to a pulp, spread out on a board and wrought and dried with great care till it resembled a coarse sort of card. This was sometimes cut into pieces about the size of the leaves of a book and upon these, with a reed cut in the shape of a pen and immersed in red or purple vegetable dye, the alphabet, syllabic and reading lessons of the spelling book and the scripture extracts usually read in the school have been neatly copied. Sometimes the whole was accurately written on one broad sheet of paper like native cloth and, after the manner of the ancients, carefully rolled up, except when used. (ibid.)

Written words assumed an enhanced sacredness when printed on Pomare's press because they were direct expressions of both sacred centrality and a European *mana* that derived, ultimately, from Jehova.

With respect to the machinery of the press itself, Hooper has suggested we might view it as

a kind of god-image – a composite and impressive object sited in a special restricted place, producing by a mysterious process materials in which god's word and power were said to reside, and which were distributed to regional shrines under the control of priests. This process paralleled in key ways those associated with the images of the deity, 'Oro, in *pa'iatua* rites. It is not surprising that Pomare was insistent on presiding over its first operation and keen to keep it in his own domains. (Hooper 2006: 64)

However, I do not think the press would have been widely understood in Tahiti or Mo'orea as a 'god-image'. Nor do I agree with Hooper when he too closely equates sheets of paper with 'red feathers brought to the main shrine, transformed/printed and redistributed' (ibid.: 75n24). Paper was not brought to the shrine by local chiefs as feathers were in the *pa'iatua* rites. Rather, I suggest that the practical equivalences were more general: like sacred feathers, sacred words printed on paper and distributed from a single sacred centre materialized a hierarchy that had Pomare and Jehova at the apex: The centripetal movement of books was perfectly balanced by the centrifugal force of their words.

Prior to the establishment of the press most, if not all, the district and sub-district chiefs in Mo'orea and Tahiti had copies of a Tahitian spelling book and/or scriptures given to them when, in 1814, they formally abandoned *marae* sacrifice and switched their allegiance to Pomare's God, becoming *Bure Atua* (Davies 1961: 172). Seven hundred copies of the spelling book, *Te Aebi no Tahiti,* had been printed in London in 1810 and 2,500 copies of a collection of scriptures and hymns, *Parau no Tahiti,* had been printed in Sydney in 1813 (Bicknell et al. to LMS, 13 Aug 1816, SSL; Lingenfelter 1967: 2, 9; Griffin 1827: 178). Pomare and the missionaries' first Tahitian printing of almost 3,000 copies of *Te Aebi no Tahiti* in 1817 doubled the number of books in circulation, most of the new copies probably being sought by people who were not of chiefly status but who were instead following chiefly precedence. In Bourdieu's terms, books had become a highly valued form of symbolic capital and the ability to read them essential cultural capital. Books became 'the most valuable property in these islands … and the most valuable gifts they [could] bestow on others (David Darling, 29 Sept 1818, in QC I: 447–48). While the missionaries intended to only distribute books to those who could read, it became normal practice to give bundles of books to local chiefs who applied for them and received them on behalf of others (Ellis 1832 III: 8; Davies, 27 Aug 1818, SSJ). Davies complained that 'because there was honour [*mana*] connected with the disposal of books they had been divided into parcels for the *raatiras* [chiefs] of the different districts *not regarding in the least the number of readers or even inhabitants*' (Davies, 4 June 1818, SSJ; emphasis added).

A central feature of the iconoclastic performances through which pre-Christian fetishes and ritual centres were destroyed was the public unbinding and unwrapping of fetishes. In the production of printed texts a corresponding significance was accorded their binding with sacredness-containing bark-cloth. Initially, two Tahitian women were employed at the press to beat bark-cloth for the covers and to dye it red and purple, while another two women folded and sewed the bindings. But the huge demand for the books soon made this impractical and binding was taken over by local specialists in the home settlements. Binding books in settlements across Tahiti and Moʻorea extended the process of fetish production from the press to the village – from centre to periphery – further contributing to the materialisation of a new, more totalized, social field. The binding of books took place under chiefly direction: 'each principal chief sent a man to learn to bind books; those who learnt charged others' (Crowl 2008: 88; see Ellis 1829a: 400–401). In addition to binding, most people made a bag or basket to carry their books in. Ellis wrote that some were afraid to take their books out of their bags 'lest they should become dirted [*sic*] or torn; afraid also to leave it at home lest it should be injured in their absence' (Ellis to LMS, 1 June 1817, in QC I: 481–91). Bark cloth tore easily and had to be protected from the rain. The fact that it was used to bind books instead of European cloth, widely available at the time, suggests that utility was less important than symbolic significance in this case.

Reflecting on the Tahitian *paʻiatua* rite, Kaeppler has proposed that it was a 'combination of the product and process of fabrication and wrapping' that made god-images sacred (2007: 97). Furthermore, the wooded core of many images were, she suggests, 'only incidental' to the sacredness – the most significant component of the image was the wrapping:

> I believe that the so-called 'wrapping' refers to layers of bark cloth and/or pandanus leaves which were also sacred owing to the prayers that had been chanted during the dressing and undressing of the sennit *toʻo*. (ibid.: 108)

The bark cloth coverings were attached to the sacred texts with bindings made from leather. In 1817, the mission printers requested a supply of animal skins from Sydney, noting that almost all of the local cats, dogs and goats had been slaughtered for their hides, which could be seen stretched out to dry in villages throughout Tahiti and Mo'orea (Davies and Ellis to LMS, 6 Dec 1817).

The sociality within this transformed social field was, however, strongly disapproved of by the missionaries. In 1818, frustrated at their inability to impose their protestant ethic of hard work and restraint in Ra'iatea, the local missionaries grumbled:

> Their 'employments' are going to the place where they are taught to read. They have native school masters throughout the whole of these islands who of their ownselves go about and teach the people, going into the bush and then praying, attending also the place of worship after which they lay down and sleep. When we tell them the necessity of working they laugh at us ... all go when they please as they please, learn, sit and talk when they please and go when they feel inclined. (Threlkeld and Williams to LMS, 30 Oct 1818, SSL)

Confirming Turner's model of ritual process, however, this literate *communitas* would soon become literate hierarchy as printed laws were nailed to church doors and local missionary societies printed rules requiring contributions of coconut oil and arrowroot.

In 1820, Ra'iatean teachers were sent, with books, westward to the Cook Island of Aitutaki. The following year, the people of Aitutaki emulated the actions of their Society Island neighbours and exchanged their *marae* fetishes for books. As noted in the introduction to this chapter, a perceived equivalence between *marae* fetishes and texts was clearly evident in the performances that immediately followed the burning of god-houses on the *marae*:

> The whole population then came in procession, district after district, the chief and priest leading the way, and people following them, bearing their rejected idols, which they laid at the teachers' feet, and then received from them in return a few copies of the gospels and elementary books. (Williams 1839: 74–75)

Formal processions were featured throughout eastern Polynesia when new *marae* were consecrated or when the social order was periodically re-constituted through *pa'iatua* in Tahiti, *luakini* rites in Hawai'i and *takurua* in the Southern Cook Islands. The staging of such a procession prior to the exchange of fetish-objects similarly signalled the inauguration of a new political order. When the LMS missionary John Williams returned to the island less than a year after this event, locals waved their spelling books above their heads to signal from the shore that they had become Christian and that the visitors would be welcomed (Williams 1839: 59; Williams to Ellis, 1 Oct 1823, SSL).

The Christian texts were also understood as god-image substitutes in Rarotonga and Atiu when Ra'iatean teachers introduced them there. When Papeiha, one of the Ra'iatean teachers from Aitutaki, was left at Rarotonga by Williams in 1823, his only possessions, besides the clothes on his back, were his gospel and a bundle of spelling books (Williams 1839: 103; Ellis 1844: 263). The books were distributed by two local priests to the high-chiefs, their families and chiefly allies who 'desired to own them above all else' (Maretu 1983: 56). Papeiha's gospel was regarded as a powerful object, perhaps equivalent to a local god-image, its pages appearing to flash in the wind 'and even though it was parcelled together it still shone brilliantly' (Maretu 1983: 58; Gill 1856: 56). Spelling books were initially used for ritual chanting rather than as tools for literate communication; when English missionaries arrived in 1827 they reported that no person was able to read (E. Pitman to My much esteemed friend, SSL). In 1828, printed sheets were sent from Huahine and the Rarotongans, like the Society Islanders a few years previously, sewed and bound them using wood and skin of cats, dogs and goats (Crowl 2008: 94).

When Ra'iatean teachers arrived at Atiu by accident in 1824, having been blown off course by a storm, their survival at sea was attributed by the people of Atiu to their books – protective fetishes that contained the power of Jehova (Williams 1839: 95; Tyerman and Bennett to LMS, 12 Nov 1824, in QC III: 140). Within a year, however, the entire population of Atiu had abandoned Christianity and rebuilt their *marae*. At this time, they returned their books to their Ra'iatean teachers, claiming that 'because of this word' the taro would not grow and the sun dried up the water (Bourne n.d.: 268).

In Hawai'i, where the history of printing generally paralleled that of church construction, texts initially had minimal or no fetishistic significance. Later, however, after 1825, texts, like churches, became a means for the imposition of a new Christian order under the direction of Ka'ahumanu and her new priests. The difference in timing between Hawai'i and the societies of eastern Polynesia was due very largely to the different levels of support for literacy by the kings or high-chiefs. Pomare was highly literate in 1817 when the press was established; Liholiho was not at all literate in 1821 and did not support mass literacy at this time. He needed to be taught the art before the masses, but he was not an enthusiastic scholar (Tyerman and Bennet 1841: 121).

And initially, between 1822 and 1825, the practices of reading and writing – termed *palapala* – were considered an art-form, an addition to other forms of chiefly amusement and entertainment. The term *palapala* originally denoted the stamping of designs on bark cloth or, as a noun, the designs and marks themselves. The missionary Bingham proposed a direct connection between the earlier and later *palapala* as the 'chosen work of the higher female chiefs':

Almost from the coming of the American missionaries in 1820 these exalted dames had generally ceased to beat or rather decorate kappa for amusement and betaken themselves to the more difficult task of learning to read and write with new letters brought by these foreign teachers. (Quoted in Schutz 1994: 155)

Actually, the transition was not as total as Bingham suggested because women did continue to decorate bark-cloth after the introduction of literacy. However, the association of literacy with the work of women may have contributed to Liholiho's lack of interest in the first printing. While in Mo'orea the first printing had been an event of national significance, Liholiho did not attend the Hawaiian event. Instead, Ka'ahumanu's brother, Keeaumoku, stood in for him. On 7 January 1822, '[He] applied the strength of his athletic arm to the lever of a Ramage press, pleased thus to assist in working off a few impressions of the first lessons' (Bingham 1981: 156). Liholiho and a number of other chiefs visited the press some days later.

Before 1825, the materials used in teaching consisted of loose pages rather than books (Dibble 1909: 249). In fact, only sixteen pages of elementary lessons and forty hymns were printed between 1822 and 1825 (ibid.; Schutz 1994: 165). The first classes were gatherings of chiefs and their immediate attendants, or as one local wrote in a letter a few years later:

The class of the community particularly devoted to books and instruction were formerly an idle train who followed the King from place to place and spent their time in foolish plays and games. (Anonymous letter quoted in Orme 1827: 93)

But it was not simply the so-called 'idle train' interested in the new art. From 1822 the chiefs, foremost among them Ka'ahumanu's brother, Kuakini and the king himself were dedicating time to it.

After 1825, the *palapala* was transformed from a chiefly pastime into a ritual practice of mass allegiance to the new chiefly order. A vast system of schools was created and competitive examination festivals involving entire islands were staged towards the end of the *makahiki* period. Popular demand for portions of the Bible (*palapala hemolele*, literally "perfect and virtuous writings") printed from 1828 onwards far outstripped supply (Schutz 1994: 167, 200; Dibble 1909: 249). Sahlins has argued convincingly that the Christian schools were 'conceived by higher Hawaiian authorities as instruments of rule and were thus encompassed in the system of land control and personal service to the *ali'i*' (1992: 93). Many of the 'teachers' at district schools were *konohiki*, local chiefs who were stewards of the land under the *mana* of an *ali'i*. A system of allegiance, grounded in commoner and chiefly *habitus,* was developed, as Dibble explained:

To whatever district a teacher [often a *Konohik*i] was sent [by an *aliʻi*] all the inhabitants of that district were expected to attend school. There was no physical compulsion, but they were told that such was 'the thought of the chief' and that was 'the right course'. What less could have been said to them? And yet these phrases amounted in their minds to law. (1909: 247)

The school buildings themselves were far from grand – 'a structure of poles and sticks thatched with leaves or grass' and without floors or furniture of any kind (ibid.: 248). But by the mid 1830s more than five hundred of them were in daily use throughout the islands (Bingham 1981: 470).

Annual examination festivals were grand occasions, held at one or two centres on each island: Oahu schools met at Honolulu, those in southwest Hawaiʻi met at Kailua while those in the north met at Hilo. Dibble wrote that 'the convocations were immense and they furnished a kind of excitement to the mass of the people filling, in a measure, a blank which had been made by the abolition of ancient festivals and public sports' (ibid.: 250). Kamakau wrote that the Oahu festival was held in April, but in 1830 Bingham attended the Hawaiʻi island festivals in mid January. Irrespective of their exact timing, these large, socially totalizing, rites must have been of a similar magnitude to the *makahiki* celebrations.

Conclusion: Binding Societies

The association between Bibles and kings had become well established elsewhere by the time of the Polynesian iconoclasm. On the frontpiece of the Great Bible, printed by Henry VIII with his new press in 1537, the king is depicted seated on his throne:

> The Bible is labelled 'Verbum Dei' and verbal scrolls circulate among the exchanges portraying Henry and his church handing the Word of God on to their various charges. At the bottom of the frontpiece, the commoners shout 'Vivet Rex'. (Spolsky 2009: 305)

Initiating a nation-wide programme intended to replace church images with books, a royal injunction, issued in 1538, required parish authorities to remove cult images from their churches and set up, instead, 'one book of the Whole Bible' in 'some convenient place' (ibid.: 306). Thus the king's image, together with God's word, were to be distributed throughout the realm.

Moreover, Bibles subsequently played an important role in the process of royal succession. On her way to her coronation twenty-one years later, Elizabeth I passed beneath a tableau on which the Bible was displayed:

A Bible in English, richly covered, was let down to her by a silk lace from a child that represented Truth. She kissed both her hands, with both her hands she received it, then she kissed it, afterwards applied it to her breast. (Cressy 1986: 97)

The kissing of the Bible had its precedence in the practice of swearing on holy relics. By the seventeenth century, defendants in the king's courts were also required to 'kiss the book' and swear an oath of truth in its presence. The book did not need to be opened (or read) – its power to enforce truth was acknowledged and amplified through kissing and placing hands on the cover (Cressey 1986: 98).

As sources of power from outside society, religious texts in central Polynesia might also be likened to the divine Fijian whale-teeth (*tabua*) of western Polynesia. Writing of the latter, Sahlins noted perceptively: 'As an object or being from beyond society that is able to generate its main relationships, the whale tooth is in such (Durkheimian) respects divine' (1983: 74). He added:

What is truly powerful are things and beings that are able to subsist beyond the bounds of society which for ordinary men is the necessary condition of their existence. Moreover, it would only be from this transcendental position that god could make society. (ibid.: 74n4)

As books replaced *marae* fetishes across eastern Polynesia during the years 1813–1824, missionaries, chiefs and thousands of ordinary people participated in the production and binding of new social relations. The production and exchange of books that contained the Word of God, printed and distributed by missionaries under the authority of Pomare was, as it had been in England, the production of a new moral order. Moreover, it was a moral order legitimated by the sacred words contained within the objects through which it was practically articulated. In Hawai'i, the printing, distribution and use of pages of scripture in schools after 1825 were critical to the integration of a new Christian chiefly order.

It seems to me that we might extend this interpretation into a general theory of fetishism that builds on the insights of Hocart, Gell and, especially, Graeber as discussed earlier. Fetishism is, I suggest, most productively viewed, not as a mode of thought, mistaken or otherwise (Ellen 1988), but as a subset of socially creative practices centred on the production, distribution and exchange of objects that appear to contain power. Fetishism can be viewed as a mode of ritual agency, a means of producing and binding new social relations through objects that internalize an external power – apparently through their construction and practically through their participation in social life. Other, closely related creative social practices that might be included in the same subset are the construction of sacred buildings such as churches.

In eastern and central Polynesia the appropriation of foreign *mana*, embodied in missionary books and churches, followed a related logic to the domestication of the chief who ritually totalized society from without in the guise of a 'stranger-king' (Sahlins 1985). As fetish objects, books and pages of scripture were, like the chiefs, containers of *mana*. They were, if you will excuse the pun, the stranger-things of stranger-kings. Book fetishism participated in what we might term, following Sahlins (1985), a 'heroic' transformation of eastern Polynesian society – in this case, the centralization of power through ritual means. We have seen that the initial destruction of *marae* and the desecration of images followed a seasonal logic and that the construction of large churches partially emulated the ritual re-building of chiefly temples. These, like the production and distribution of religious books were centralizing practices through which chiefly *mana* was transformed into the power of kings. Social transformation could then proceed further via the proclamations of laws that were legitimized with reference to the printed words of Jehova.

In the Cook Islands and the Society Islands printed texts also became quasi-imperial objects in that they bound 'outer' islands to the centres of power. The printing and distribution of biblical texts (translated into Rarotongan) throughout the southern and northern Cook Islands would lay the foundations for present-day nationhood in that the Rarotongan language and dialect thus became a *lingua franca* (Sissons 1999). In 1821, Pomare extended his supreme ritual authority (*hau*) to the Austral Islands, bringing together two divisions of Ra'ivavae that had been engaged in protracted military conflict and precipitating an iconoclasm. In exchange for peace, the chiefs and people of Ra'ivavae received missionary texts and Pomare's laws. A regionally understood association between Pomare's 'empire' and the 'word' would be later affirmed in the Marquesas Islands where one of the justifications for the rejection of Christianity was that in accepting 'the word' the land 'would become the land of Pomare' (Thomas 1990: 149). As it had been during the reign of 'Oro when politics were ritually centred on Taputaputea *marae* at Ra'iatea, home of the original 'Oro image, the outer limits of empire would coincide with the outer limits of fetish distribution.

7

New Tabus and Ancient Pleasures

When in June 1824 the LMS delegation led by Messrs Tyerman and Bennet visited Atiu in the Southern Cook Islands, they were pleased to learn that the entire island had recently 'thrown away their idols', built a large chapel and 'embraced the gospel' (QC III: 140). We know, however, that soon afterwards the people of Atiu realized their mistake and returned their spelling books to their Ra'iatean teachers. The problem, as Robert Bourne recorded it in October 1825, was that the taro crop failed: 'the people say', he continued, 'it is because of this word that is come among them that the sun dries up the water' (Bourne n.d.: 268).

Bourne was unimpressed with this explanation for the smallness of the taro, but I think the speaker was intending to convey, in a metaphoric language favoured by chiefs and priests, a deeper point: an excess of foreign *tapu* (sacredness) had become a threat to life. The Christian religion with its new practices of reading and memorizing the *tapu* words of Jehova had been threatening the life of the people and their society just as the increased intensity of the sun (caused by these words) had threatened the growth of taro, a staple of life in the Southern Cook Islands. The roots of the problem were both the continuous intensity of the sun-like tabus and their foreign nature, making them unsuitable for Atiu's physical and social climate. This is, at least, a plausible interpretation of the remark and one that is supported by the argument I make in this chapter: The excesses of Christianity across eastern Polynesia in the 1820s and 1830s most crucially included an abolition of a seasonality of power that could only be restored through a return to the *communitas* of Pleiades above.

The imposition of the new Christian tabus that underpinned a Christian hierarchy and their rejection by those who found them oppressive followed the seasonal logic of *communitas* and hierarchy that I introduced in Chapter 1. Sahlins has already shown that this was the case in Hawai'i – the issuing of new Christian moral commands by Kamehameha's widow Ka'ahumanu took place there during her circuits of islands at a time when the Ku temples would previously have been re-opened and rebellions typically occurred during the *makahiki* season – and I will argue that this was also generally so across eastern Polynesia. The imposition of Christian tabus in the form of biblically based laws and commandments and rigid body tabus undermined a fundamental seasonality in that continuous obedience to laws was expected and enforced. From a pre-Christian perspective this was clearly overdoing the tabuing.

Rebellions, cultural revivals and rejections of Christian restrictions typically occurred during the season of Pleiades above and were thus re-assertions of a seasonality of power. Moreover, they were bodily rejections expressed through dancing, sex, sports, tattooing and feasting, sacred activities previously directed towards attracting the gods and thus ensuring abundance, fertility and the continuity of life itself. Excessive hierarchy had always been a threat to life and fertility – that is why certain priests and chiefs hid themselves during the revelries of Pleiades above – and now everywhere this threat was recognized in the form of Christian excess. A shared seasonal logic of ritual totalization and shared dispositions to oppose excessive hierarchy with bodily excesses help explain, I suggest, a common regional response to Christianity in the 1820s and 1830s.

I begin this chapter with an account of the imposition of legal and moral codes in Tahiti, the Leeward Islands, Rarotonga and Hawai'i, highlighting the timing of their introduction and the practices of priestly and chiefly judgement with which they were associated. This is followed by a discussion of three episodes of significant rebellion against Christian laws and restrictions, all of which occurred during the season of Pleiades above: in Tahiti and Ra'iatea in 1823–1824; in Rarotonga in 1830–1832; and in Hawai'i in 1832–1834. The denial of seasonality clearly coincided with the creation of a more individualizing form of power. With the introduction of laws, the written word became, like the large, hierarchical churches, a new technology of priestly and chiefly control; laws gave former priests and chiefs license to meddle more in the lives of individual commoners. But while it is useful to distinguish different forms of governmentality as Foucault did, a genealogical understanding is simply incapable of explaining their emergence. Practice history reveals how they *and resistances to them* are always the product of strategic improvisations upon pre-existing practices.

New Tabus of Pleiades Below

As we have seen, on 13 May 1819, some three and a half years after he had ordered the destruction of all the remaining god-images in Tahiti and Mo'orea, high-chief Pomare ascended one of three pulpits in his recently completed Royal Mission Chapel. The pulpit was on the eastern side of the building. This side was associated with life and male *mana* and it was also, according to Ellis, considered the 'court side' of the chapel. Beneath Pomare, seated on matting, were some six thousand to seven thousand people, virtually the entire population of Tahiti. Standing beside the high-chief in the pulpit, one of his new priests, William Crook, offered a prayer, read from 'a suitable portion' of the Bible and implored the sanction of the King of Kings upon the proceedings that were to follow' (Ellis 1834 II: 378; 1832 III: 139). Pomare began by addressing Tati, chief of the Papara district and brother of the late Opufara:

> 'Tati', said the king, 'what is your desire? What can I do for you?' Tati, who sat nearly opposite the pulpit arose and said, 'Those are what we want – the papers you hold in your hand – the laws; give them to us that we may have them in our hands, that we may regard them and do what is right.' (Ellis 1832 III: 139)

Pomare then addressed the same questions to other district leaders and received from them similar responses. He then proceeded to read the eighteen articles of a code of laws written by himself and the LMS missionary, Henry Nott, commenting on each clause in turn and concluding with the appointment of judges, chief of whom was Tati. Mass approval was signalled through the raising of thousands of hands, this creating a remarkable rushing noise (ibid.: 140).

Pomare had become a new kind of stranger-king, his *mana*, like that of the British monarch, now derived from Jehova. Sahlins's description of the socially creative role of the stranger-king is strikingly apt here:

> To be able to put society in order the king must first reproduce an original disorder. Having committed his monstrous acts against society, proving he is stronger than it, the ruler proceeds to bring system out of chaos. Recapitulating the initial constitution of social life, the accession of the king is the recreation of the universe. (Sahlins 1985: 80)

Codes of law, similar to that of Pomare and Nott, were later introduced for Ra'iatea, Taha'a, Borabora (1820) and Huahine (1822), and with the exception of Borabora, all of the ceremonies took place at the beginning of the season of Pleiades below and after the opening of churches. At Ra'iatea, the new large chapel, consecrated on 11 April 1820, included a courthouse partitioned off at one end (LMS delegation report, in QC II: 427). At the public gathering of almost the entire population held the next day, laws based on but extending those proclaimed in Tahiti, were read out and approved and judges were appointed (Ellis 1832 III: 143–44; Ellis 1844 I: 145). Because the Ra'iatea high-chief, Tamatoa, was also *ari'i* for Taha'a, Borabora and Maupiti, these laws were also considered to have been proclaimed for the latter islands (Davies 1961: 372; Ellis 1832 III: 143). Two weeks later, on the last Sunday of the month, seventy people, including the principal chiefs and their households, were baptized:

The candidates were seated in front of the pulpit ... great attention and apparent seriousness pervaded the assembly ... the adults retained their names when these were not improper; but new names, principally Scripture names, were given to the children. (Prout 1846: 31)

Church consecration, law proclamation and baptism of chiefly families were thus strongly linked as rites of hierarchy enacted at the beginning of *matariʻi-i-raro,* Pleiades below.

The large, new Huahine chapel was also opened in May 1820, but the public proclamation of laws was delayed until May 1822 (Davies 1961: 299; Ellis 1832 III: 175). They were written by missionaries, William Ellis and Henry Nott, and approved by the high-chief of Huahine prior to their proclamation. There were thirty in total and they dealt with the following: murder, theft, pigs in gardens, receiving stolen goods, exchange of goods, disregard of the Sabbath, rebellion, polygamy, adultery, marriage, support duties of a husband, impossibility of divorce, false accusations, unnatural sex, seduction, rape, sex outside marriage, drunkenness, dangerous dogs and hogs, pig hunting, conspiracy, informing on a crime, unauthorized climbing of trees for food, beachcombing without reporting finds of value, taxes, tattooing, appropriate voyaging behaviour, bribing judges and the revision of laws. The penalty for murder and repeated rebellion was banishment to an uninhabited island. 'Unnatural sex' called for 'perpetual banishment or incessant hard labour for seven years'. Theft required compensation of four times the amount stolen, half to the owner and half to the king. The punishments for disregarding the Sabbath, seduction, sex outside marriage, drunkenness, unauthorized climbing for food and tattooing were to construct sections of a public road of varying lengths (for men) or cloth-making (for women). With reference to laws requiring payment of taxes – these in the form of pigs, arrowroot, coconut and mats – Newbury noted that:

the missionaries aimed at codifying and rationalizing the ceremonial exchange of surplus. But they prohibited the festive occasions that had formerly marked such exchanges; and they made it clear annual taxation was a recognition of the power of civil authority – frequently inculcated in the Word of God. (Davies 1961: 369)

Ellis was immensely proud of his and Nott's laws and included an English translation of them in his *Polynesian Researches* (Ellis 1832 III: 177–92).

Although the unwrapping and re-wrapping of god-images and the renewal of sacred feathers attached to them had been performed by priests out of the sight of commoners, this *paʻiatua* rite, performed throughout the Society Islands in April and May, had in fact required the active participation of the entire population. The people's role had been to bring offerings for the gods, priests and high-chief. These had included chiefly foods such as pigs, deep-sea fish and turtles, together with woven mats, rolls of bark-cloth and feather garments (Henry 1928: 174–75). After presenting their offerings, groups of people, each headed by their chief, had assembled in the outer courtyard of a recently weeded and restored *marae* to be formally dismissed by a priest standing in an area above them. He told them that the world was now free of pollution and fault (*aia'ai*) – inland and seaward, above and below, in the *Po* (world of gods and ancestors) –and in this world of the living, order had been restored (Henry 1928: 175; Babadzan 1993: 48).

The seasonal practice of gathering entire populations at major *marae* to witness priestly proclamations of renewed order was partially replicated in the proclamation of laws. At the beginning of the season of Pleiades below and within a recently created sacred space, people assembled to participate in a renewal of power and life. Order was proclaimed to the assenting masses and their chiefs by a high-chief, visibly supported by his priests. In the new circumstances the order proclaimed was not that of 'Oro or Tane but would instead to be based on written words representing the commandments of Jehova. Jehova's priests opened and closed the proceedings and stood beside the *ari'i* as they read the laws. Offerings of food and cloth to the *ari'i* and the mission had been made at the consecrations of the new churches and all districts of each island had contributed labour and materials. The return 'gift', like that which had been sought through the priests of 'Oro and Tane, would be life itself, secured through actions that were now in accordance with the true cosmological order of things.

In addition to proclaiming codes of law, Pomare and the high-chiefs of the Society Islands appointed judges. In most cases the chief judges were former high-priests, usually the younger brothers of high-chiefs. At Tahiti, the chief judge was Tati, younger brother of Pomare's main rival, Opufara, killed by Pomare's Christian forces in November 1815 (Davies 1961: 368). At Ra'iatea, the chief judge, Pahi, was the younger brother of King Tamatoa (Tyerman and Bennet 1841: 27, 32, 156; Davies 1961: 368) and in Mo'orea the former head priest, Pati'i was appointed chief judge (Tyerman and Bennet 1841: 27, 32; QC II: 156-7, 425–26; Ellis 1844 II: 206). As we saw in Chapter 2, Pahi and Pati'i had been the first on their respective islands to destroy their god-images in 1814, setting a precedent for the general iconoclasm which followed.

Priests (*tahua'a pure*) and high-priests (*tahua'a rahi*) were learned men and experts in public performance. They were skilled at all forms of prayer, including those that animated god-images, repelled sorcery or ensured the effective restraint of prisoners. They were experts at persuasive political performance and oratory that included colourful metaphor. They learned how to declare war and sue for peace (Henry 1928: 154–55). They were highly respected, but also much feared – 'their curse could bring sickness or death' (ibid. 292).

'Judging', then, would be improvised and performed by men whose godly *habitus* was well suited to the new practice. These were also men who had a 'taste' for ritual and public performance and all that went with it – dressing up, being at the centre of attention, being both respected and feared. These were men who already embodied dignity and authority and who were skilled at discovering and dealing with breaches of social order. Embodied as *habitus* was a disposition to practically synchronize cosmological and social orders.

Court sessions and judges were both termed *ha'ava* in Tahitian, translated as 'judging' by the missionaries (Crook, March 23 1821, SSJ; Davies 1851). *Ha'a* is a causative and *va* means a deluge or dumping of rain. Literally, then, *ha'ava* was the bringing down of a deluge – and in this case it both cleansed and punished – or it was the person performing this action. It is what gods, priests and high-chiefs did when responding to breaches of *tapu* by commoners (Ellis 1832 III: 123).

Here is an episode of *ha'ava* as witnessed in Tahiti and described by Captain Beechy in 1832:

> The court was ranged upon benches placed in successive rows under trees, with the prisoners in front under the charge of an officer with a drawn sabre and habited in a volunteer's jacket and maro [a loin-cloth]. The aava-rai [*ha'ava rahi*, head judge] of the district in which the crimes had been committed took his place between the court and the prisoners, dressed in a long straw mat, finely plaited and edged with fringe, with a slit cut in it for the head to pass through [a *tiputa*]; a white oakum wig which, in imitation of the gentlemen of our courts of law, flowed in long curls over his shoulders, and a tall cap [head-dress] surmounting it, curiously ornamented with red feathers and with variously coloured tresses of human hair [*tamau*]. (Beechy 1832: 187–88; See D'Alleva 2001 for a speculative interpretation of Tahitian tamau as objectifications of genealogy)

The white wig appears to have been a recent innovation – it did not feature in any earlier accounts of episodes in Tahiti in 1820 or Mo'orea in 1821. In 1820 LMS missionary William Crook described a judge wearing 'a headdress of feathers, principally red, which they formerly wore at their idolatrous rites' (30 Oct 1820, SSJ). In 1821, at Mo'orea, the visiting delegation from the LMS saw judges wearing *tiputa* and straw hats. The hat of the chief judge was 'distinguished above the rest by a bunch of black feathers gracefully surmounted with red (Tyerman and Bennet 1841: 48).

Tiputa (ponchos) and headdresses were priestly and chiefly items of dress. Henry records that the *tiputa* worn by men of rank were of red, black and yellow feathers (Henry 1928: 285). Thomas concludes, rightly in my view, that they were probably only worn by people of high rank because commoners were required to present themselves bare-chested before high-chiefs and priests (Thomas 2003: 85). Red feathers, which we know were particularly sacred in pre-Christian Tahiti, were also a feature of chief's and priest's headdresses. Those worn by the judges appear to have been of a commonly worn type termed *taupoʻo* (Henry 1928: 285–86).

During their visit to Raʻiatea in November 1822, the LMS delegation witnessed a trial at which Pahi, the former iconoclastic head priest and brother of Tamatoa, was the judge:

> [Pahi] was gorgeously attired in his official cap [headdress] and robe of feathers. On either hand of him were sixteen local officers who have two and two the civil superintendence of the eight districts into which the island is divided. Each of these, as the symbol of authority, held in his hand a printed copy of the laws, rolled up and inclosed [*sic*] in a joint of bamboo. The jury consisted of six persons of well-approved character. (Tyerman and Bennet 1841: 137)

'Judgings' in the early years were not trials at which the guilt or innocence of an accused was determined through cross-examination. Almost all prisoners confessed their guilt immediately upon being accused and the visiting LMS delegation was assured that 'confession [was] so common as to constitute a trait of national character' (ibid.: 48). This was indeed an expression of commoner *habitus* – not to confess would have been to show a lack of humility and respect for the rank of the judge. The LMS delegation further commented:

> It is remarkable in the administration of justice here that when a sentence is pronounced the criminal is gravely asked whether he himself agrees to it and he generally replies in the affirmative. There is something very primitive and patriarchal in this simple yet solemn form of conducting trials. (ibid.)

A priestly *habitus* of authority and solemnity matched by a commoner *habitus* of humility and respect imbued structure and direction to the improvised proceedings, each a new re-enactment of chiefly hierarchy.

In the early years of 'judging', sentences varied considerably depending on the whim of the judge, the status of the defendant and the nature of the offense as understood in its broadest social context. In the 1826 trial witnessed by Captain Beechy, the prisoner had stolen an item of clothing from a European resident. He was admonished and fined four pigs – two to be given to Pomare and two to be given to the owner of the clothing as specified in the laws. In the earlier 1821 trial witnessed by the LMS delegation at Moʻorea the prisoners were two young men who had stolen some breadfruit. In admonishing them, the judge told them 'they had committed rebellion by breaking the law, outraging the authority of the King [Pomare] and disgracing the character of their country' (Tyerman and Bennet 1841: 48). Each was sentenced to build part of a wall around Pomare's taro plot, although their friends and relatives could help them in this task.

It might seem extraordinary that the theft of a few breadfruit could have been spoken of as 'rebellion'. But 'rebellion' (*'orure hau*) had been the general term for a wide range of punishable offenses against hierarchy in pre-Christian Tahiti; these included challenging a chief's rank, withholding tribute or speaking contemptuously about a high-chief. In all such cases chiefs were expected to react with force in order to uphold their *mana* (Ellis 1832 III: 123). It appears, then, that now all offenses against Pomare's new laws, even the theft of some breadfruit, were understood to be offenses against the high-chief himself and the god he represented.

New Tabus in Rarotonga and Hawai'i

We have seen that after the Rarotongan iconoclasm during the season of Pleiades above, the supporters of the district high-chiefs moved *en masse* to Avarua, the present-day capital in the Te Au-o-tonga district. As Pleiades dipped below the horizon in May of 1823 people began work on a very large church, partly in emulation of Pomare. It was still under construction and only 300 feet in length when the LMS delegation visited the island in June (Tyerman and Bennet 1841: 179). Three years later, soon after the arrival of the missionaries John Williams and Charles Pitman, the Avarua Christians all moved to the adjacent district of Takitumu. Here, again in May, they began work on another chapel, decorating it in early June with bark-cloth wrappings from one of the images that belonged to the Te Au-o-tonga district (Pitman to LMS, 6 Nov 1827, SSL). Perhaps this was to emphasize the socially totalizing nature of the building intended to unite, if only temporarily, both districts.

Immediately after completing this chapel the entire Christian population moved back to Avarua where, some six weeks later, a great assembly of all the chiefs proclaimed new laws based on those adopted at Ra'iatea (Maretu 1983: 81n4; Gill 1856: 31). The missionaries stressed in their official correspondence that these laws, like those of Ra'iatea, had been requested by the chiefs, thus pretending that they had not interfered in the government of the island. Pitman stressed his reluctance to become involved but argued that only he and Williams, as outside priests, could have produced effective laws:

> By their request we have established a code of laws for them similar
> to the Tahitian with a few exceptions and additions of others (which

would not apply to these islands). It was not my intention to have anything to do with their political concerns but as some laws for the regulation of people were absolutely necessary and it would not have been regarded had it been done by the chiefs, I agreed ... Mr Wms translated and drew up the laws which were read to the chiefs and people in a public meeting and met with their approbation. (Pitman to LMS, 6 Nov 1827, SSL)

In addition to proclaiming laws, Christian judges were appointed and, for all district subdivisions (tapere), two 'custodians of the laws' and two 'police-men' were appointed to put the laws into practice. The chief judge was a man named Tupe, a former leading priest and younger brother of Pa, the *ariki* of the Takitumu district (Maretu 1983: 44n43, 87). He had, in the two years pre-viously, been a leader of a thousand-strong army of traditional warriors that had been organized to defend the *ariki* from those opposed to the adoption of Jehova as the national god.

There are no accounts of trials for this period, but we know that the Ra'iat-ean jury system had been adopted and it is likely that they followed a similar procedure to that in Ra'iatea. Williams included in his *Narrative* an illustration of a magnificent head-dress from the nearby island of Aitutaki that bears the caption: 'A cap from Aitutaki, worn formerly by the master of ceremonies at native dances; but now by the chief judge of the island' (Williams 1839: 537; see Figure 7.1). The modified Ra'iatean laws were adopted in Aitutaki soon after the proclamation of laws in Rarotonga and it appears that the practice of judging there was also placed under the control of former priests.

In Hawai'i, prior to 1825, instruction in the practices of reading and writ-ing – *palapala* – had been largely confined to the chiefly elite. But in April 1824, some three months after the King had departed for England and when the process of re-opening the Ku temples would normally have begun, a coun-cil of chiefs and missionaries announced their intention to extend the *palapala* and the word of God to the common people (Mykkanen 2003: 49; Dibble 1909: 204). In June the following year, after a rebellion in Kaua'i had been successfully put down with the assistance of the missionaries' prayers, an edict requiring the building of and attendance at schools was proclaimed by Ka'ahu-manu. Now the effective head of the government, she and others of the ruling elite were baptized in December 1825.

Ka'ahumanu and island governors supported by missionaries soon began making circuits of the islands announcing the necessity to comply with new Christian tabus – and the concept of *kapu* was explicitly invoked in this con-text (Sahlins 1992: 72). Here is how the missionary, Rev. Sheldon Dibble, de-scribed the circuits:

Kaahumanu and other high chiefs made repeated tours around all the principal islands – around Oahu, Kauai, Molokai, Maui and Hawaii,

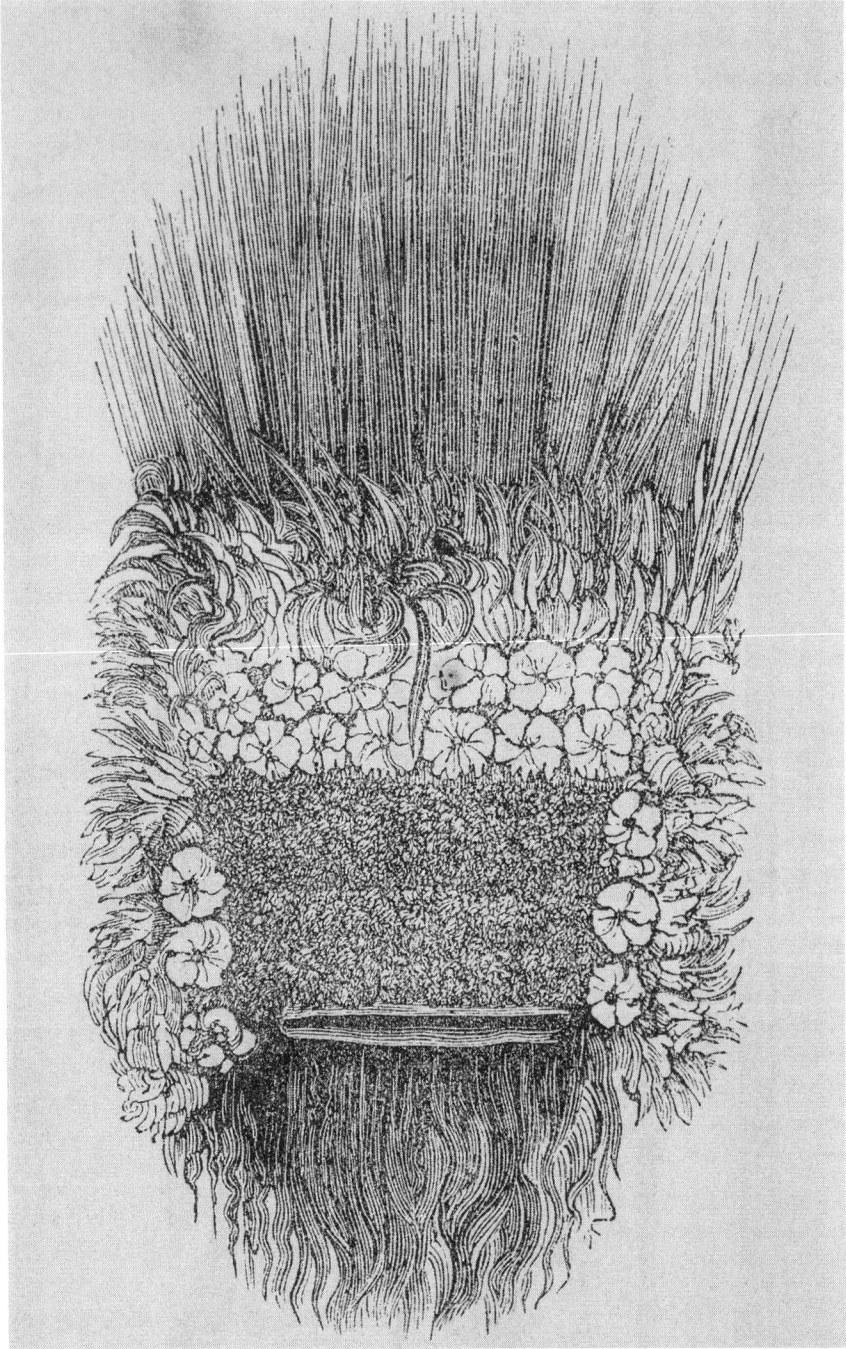

Figure 7.1. A priest's or chief's headdress worn by a judge in Christian Aitutaki. *Source:* Engraving from Williams (1838). Victoria University of Wellington.

assembling the people from village to village and delivering addresses day after day in which they prohibited immoral acts, enjoined the observance of the Christian Sabbath, encouraged the people to learn to read and exhorted them to turn to God and to love and obey the Saviour of sinners … The people were not only accustomed to obey without inquiry or hesitation but were also in the habit of complying at once with every wish or the least intimation of desire or choice on the part of the chiefs … The effect was electrical, pervading at once every island of the group, every obscure village and district and operating with immense power on all grades and conditions of society. The chiefs gave orders to the people to erect houses of worship, to build school-houses and to learn to read – they readily did so. (Dibble 1909: 205–6)

Just as it had in the Society and Southern Cook Islands, where the proclamation of written laws had taken place after the opening of temples during the season of Pleiades below, the proclamations of Jehova's laws, which were the new basis of chiefly hierarchy, were performed by Ka'ahumanu with her new priests at her side. The missionary, Hiram Bingham, who accompanied Ka'ahumanu on her first circuit of Oahu, recorded that she told her people that just as God had the right to make laws and expect obedience so too did his representatives, the 'rulers' (quoted in Sahlins 1992: 71). Prohibitions against murder, theft and adultery were printed in December 1827 and were to come into force after the *makahiki* season (Kuykendall 1938: 125–26). These laws of Jehova (*ke kanawai o Iehowa*), based on interpretations of the Ten Commandments, in combination with the extension of the *palapala*, promoted an intensification of chiefly power as effectively as had the introduction of written laws in the Society and Southern Cook Islands.

Ancient Pleasures of Pleaides Above

On 22 November 1823, at the beginning of the season of Pleiades above during which hierarchies had normally been temporarily dissolved, the visiting LMS delegation was treated to a hilarious performance that ridiculed the practice of 'judging' in Tahiti. The 'prisoner' was a large man dressed in the clothing of a judge, 'gorgeously attired' in a judicial costume that included a fine *tiputa* and a brilliant feather headdress. The 'judge', in stark contrast, stood only three-feet-eight-inches tall and was entirely naked. The dwarf

> played the giant well; while the giant to his own inexpressible mortification, and the delight of the bystanders, enacted the part of the dwarf not less successfully for he felt and looked as little as even his accusers could desire. The court having heard the evidence on which a verdict

of guilty was instantly pronounced, the judge gathered himself up in all his official dignities, lectured the criminal with great but merited severity, and pronounced sentence upon him with as much justice as can consist without any mercy. (Tyerman and Bennet 1841: 166)

The missionaries considered such carnivalesque reversals and other revelries of Pleiades above to be a threat to the continuity and permanence of the new Christian order. They had already abolished Christmas because it occurred at the wrong time of year, that is, during this season, and the LMS delegation strongly advised that such performances 'be repressed' (ibid.). But after four years of such repression the wider population, including many chiefs, was in no mood to listen.

There had been earlier acts of resistance to Pomare's laws in Tahiti. In September 1819, four months after the laws had been proclaimed, Pomare's house was burned down and his life and that of the chief judge were threatened. Pomare responded by declaring war on the home district of the rebels and by later hanging the rebel leaders (Bicknell and Tessier to LMS, 6 June 1820, SSL). The following year, a few days before the May meeting in Tahiti's Royal Chapel, a large feast was held at which the future of Christianity and its laws were debated by a gathering of local chiefs. A pig was subsequently sent to Pomare from the gathering with a request that the island return to its former practices of sacrifice and worship. This time, Pomare responded by banishing the hosts of the feast from their lands and villages. The missionary William Gyles who recorded this event, commented: 'no doubt there are many who are opposed to Christianity but some not show it' (W. Gyles, 'Answers to Miscellaneous Enquiries' 1820, SSL). A further attempt was made on Pomare's life in July 1821. When Pomare learned of the plot he wrote to his new priest, William Crook, to warn him that some people opposed to the Christian laws intended to kill the missionaries and judges. However, a war, expected to involve the whole island, did not eventuate (Pomare to Crook, July 1821, in Crook letters, SSL).

The judges, with support from the missionaries, had been active in convicting large numbers of young people for fornication and tattooing. Those convicted of sexual crimes were set to work building a public road around the island, while others were employed building new churches (J. Hayward to LMS, 16 Aug 1822, SSL). By November 1823 'many young people on all islands' were defying the judges and having themselves tattooed – suffering judicial punishment became part of their rite of passage (Darling to LMS, Oct 1823, SSL). During the Pleiades above season of 1823–1824 'all the young men, with very few exceptions, became, as Crook put it, 'very wild' (Crook, 12 Dec 1823, SSJ). But it was not only the young men who became 'wild': the entire population of some districts, chiefs included, participated in dancing, feasting and tattooing. The favourite day for the latter practice was the Christian Sabbath. Church services and, as we have seen, trials were mocked (Crook, 15

Dec–26 Feb SSJ; Gunson 1962: 213). Penalties became harsher. Flogging was introduced, for example:

> I prevailed upon the judges to send the boys to school to be judged and punished there instead of being kept tied up with ropes and sent to labour on the road with those who will not fail to make them worse. They were found guilty by their own confession and punished with a dozen lashes with a cat-o-nine-tails. The teachers, some of whom are judges, inflicting the punishment, (Crook, 5 Jan 1824, SSJ)

But such practices had little effect on the cultural revivals of Pleiades above, which continued unabated. When the Russian voyager Kotzebue visited a school in March 1824, he was astonished to find 'neither lively children nor youths but adults and aged persons who crept slowly in with downcast looks and prayer books under their arms' (Barratt 1992: 192).

This revival of ancient pleasures was not confined to Tahiti but extended also to the Leeward Islands. At Ra'iatea, there had been strong opposition to Tamatoa's laws even before their proclamation in April 1820. A few weeks prior, a priest had threatened to kill John Williams and his family, causing his wife to miscarry (Williams 1839: 129–33), and in 1821 there was an armed rebellion by forty-six tattooed young men, including Tamatoa's son. In April 1822, following Pomare's death in December 1821 and in response to harsh 'judging' during the *matahiti* season, a more serious armed rebellion occurred, the intention being to 'set fire to the houses, kill all the chiefs and baptized persons and overthrow the government' (Threlkeld and Williams to LMS, 8 July 1822, SSL). The rebels fortified themselves in the hills and the whole island prepared for war. After negotiations with the judges and King Tamatoa, however, the rebels surrendered. Sentences of hanging were initially handed down to the twelve leaders, but these were later commuted to working in chains, and the rebels' lands and property were confiscated (ibid.).

While young men continued to defy the judges and have themselves tattooed, later that year the *communitas* of Pleiades above in the Leeward Islands took on quite a different character to that in Tahiti. Instead of reviving pre-Christian dances, sexual freedoms and body adornments, the people of Ra'iatea staged an elaborate parody of European culture.

On 4 December, a thousand people gathered on a coral pier for a 'picnic'. The pier was overlaid with fresh leaves and covered with a huge awning of bark-cloth. Two hundred and fifty-one sofas, each specifically made for the occasion by a household, were carried to the pier and arranged around tables:

> The tables were covered with *purau*-matting and native cloth. The utensils upon them, as may be imagined, were very miscellaneous. Those who had plates, knives, forks, spoons, crockery or metal wares of any kind which could be used in eating or drinking exhibited all

their *tana papa* (foreign property) and handled the strange things with more dexterity, but not with more good humour, than might have been expected, where each was determined to do his best and to be pleased with what his neighbours did. (Tyerman and Bennet 1841: 139)

Later in the day, a riotous 'tea ceremony' was held:

The principal supply was from a large vat, or sugar-boiler, which was brought down to the shore and filled with water slightly sweetened, but without any infusion of the Chinese plant [tea]. The variety of drinking-vessels was ludicrous – pots, plates, delf-ware, porringers, cans, glasses and even bottles; but principally cocoa-nut shells, their own native and elegantly-sculptured cups. More enjoyment with less indecorum among so numerous a company of revellers is rarely to be found in this world. (ibid.: 140)

In April 1828, some six months after the proclamation of Rarotonga's code of laws, Makea, the high chief of the island's Te Au-o-tonga district, accompanied John Williams on a visit to the Society Islands. Makea was shocked to discover the high level of missionary and judicial oppression and learned of the widespread opposition to it. Since 1826, a number of visionaries, principally Te Ao, Hue and Te Rua, had been gathering followers, claiming to be directly inspired by God and, as inspired priests had done in pre-Christian times, challenging the hierarchical order. By the time of Makea's visit these movements were being vigorously opposed by the Tahitian judges. Their leaders had been banished to Ra'iatea (which Makea also visited) and their followers were forced to walk barefoot around the reefs, swimming over the openings, as the judges walked along the shore (Gunson 1962: 221–22). While the number of followers that the visionaries attracted may not have been large, their movements were the visible tip of a deeper hostility to missionaries and their laws that Makea could not have failed to notice.

On his return to Rarotonga in August 1828, therefore, Makea wanted nothing to do with Aaron Buzacott, the missionary stationed in his district. Buzacott wrote that his conduct and that of 'nearly the whole of the people' was 'altered from respectful and obliging to that of the contrary … they began to steal our pigs and poultry, the intention of which, some of them informed us, was to drive us from the station' (Buzacott to LMS, 2 Dec 1829, SSL). By early 1829, a determined opposition to missionaries and judges developed in Rarotonga. The missionary William Gill later wrote that the movement had been led by former priests who 'resolved to die rather than submit to the Gospel', that is to the laws derived from it, and that these priests were supported by a number of 'great men of the land' (Gill 1871: 15; Gill 1856: 34). It is unclear whether this group of 'great men' included Makea, but it may have, certainly initially. Conflict reached a peak in May 1829 when the house of the chief judge, Tupe, was burned down. Buzacott wrote:

> The principal chiefs, being determined to re-establish and support the laws, it raised an opposition among some lesser chiefs who would have much rather remained lawless. They commenced their attack by secretly setting fire to the houses of judges, to the school rooms, chapel etc. The number of houses burnt in a short time amounted to no less than fifteen … nearly a hundred natives were stationed around our house. (Buzacott to LMS, 2 Dec 1829, SSL)

The conflict continued through the summer of 1829–1830, but in March 1830 a deadly epidemic, probably dysentery, spread throughout the island. All were taken ill and, tragically, around a seventh of the population died within a few months (Pitman to LMS, 2 July 1830; Buzacott to LMS, 17 Aug 1830, SSL). This devastating loss of life did not, however, send people flocking back to the churches. By 1833 there were only a total of eighty-eight baptized adults out of a population of some three to four thousand (Gill 1871: 34). Instead, it appears that Makea Ariki, Pa Ariki and many sub-district chiefs had come to the same conclusion as their neighbours in Atiu: too much Christianity and overdoing the tabuing was not good for the health.

In 1830, at the beginning of the season of Pleiades above, therefore, the chiefs initiated life-enhancing revivals of erotic dancing, feasting, tattooing and sexual freedom. Pitman wrote:

> Our chief [Pa Ariki] has turned his back on us and openly counte-nanced the evil practices of the people. When the festivities were over Pa's wife visited Pitman's wife to say that she was much ashamed of her late conduct – [Mrs Pitman] exhorted her no more to follow those evil customs which had been abolished – to which she agreed. (Pit-man to LMS, 9 Mar 1831, SSL)

At least she would hold off doing so until next summer. At the beginning of the next season of festivity in November that year a meeting of chiefs was held at Avarua at which it was agreed to once again revive the pre-Christian forms of pleasure and entertainment. Young men immediately began to have themselves tattooed and to openly criticize the missionaries; their 'chiefs coun-tenancing the people's return to their old customs emboldened many to do and say what otherwise they would not' (Pitman, 10 Dec 1831). Pitman's important journal entry for 24 November is worth quoting at length:

> Our young men are all marking themselves. This is what I have been expecting would be the case owing to the opportunity Makea the chief

of Avarua and others have of visiting the other islands in Mr Wms vessel – I have therefore to the utmost of my strength employed what time I possible could in instructing the young people that they may have a knowledge of reading etc. etc. ere they had an opportunity of following their evil desires. These things would doubtless ultimately have been the case but I have endeavoured to keep off the evil day as long as possible. *The desire of nearly all the people on the island is for their old practices being revived,* it is not from principle of love to God but because other islands have done the same. Hence when the two native teachers came here [Papeiha and Tiberio] they spoke to them of the changes in other islands, after a little opposition from some few their chiefs professed to receive the new religion but from what motive? From a conviction of its being the word of the true God? From a desire to follow the mind and will of God revealed in his word? No! but because Tahiti and Ra'iatea had embraced it – the chiefs embraced it – gave leave to abolish their old customs because the teachers said it was wrong but not from a desire to let them go – not from any love to the new system – in a word, not from principle – and should the chiefs again turn their backs to the Teachers *the people would, for the greater part by far, return with them with joy to their heathenish practices.* (ibid., emphasis added)

A parallel desire to return to 'heathenish practices' was also evident in Hawai'i. Handy speculated that without the *makahiki* festival the monotony of life would have become oppressive. Tributes to the king and chiefs by commoners were no longer investments in future bounty, made in the midst of the pageantry, seasonal dancing and great drama surrounding Lono's arrival and departure. They were, instead, 'payments in cold blood' (Handy 1931: 29). What Handy failed to notice, however, was that the *makahiki* festivities did, in fact, reappear in new guises.

Towards the end of the *makahiki* season of 1826–1827, people reasserted a seasonality of power by abandoning schools and churches and returning to dancing, sports and festivities. Ralston noted:

This desertion, which occurred at what would have been the end of the *makahiki* season, traditionally a time of festivities and license, was not long lived, but it clearly revealed that ancient patterns of thought, belief and activity had not been erased. (Ralston 1985: 318)

Ka'ahumanu and her supporters successfully overcame such challenges to their developing Christian hegemony by 1829. By the time of Ka'ahumanu's death in June 1832, a puritanical Christian order that effectively excluded King

Kauikeaouli had become firmly established. In response, during the *makahiki* season of 1832–1833, the eighteen-year-old king abrogated the new Christian tabus and, supported by a group of pleasure-loving attendants known as the *Hulumanu,* inaugurated a new period of revelry and *communitas.* Throughout the archipelago, schools and churches were abandoned and thousands participated instead in traditional games, *hula* and feasting.

The king continued his support for, and participation in, ancient pleasures throughout 1833 and 1834. Although he never directly threatened the mission, he certainly mocked it. On one occasion he had a full Christian burial service performed for a pet baboon that had been placed in a coffin (Ralston 1985: 320). In 1834, he made a circuit of Oahu in the reverse direction to that of Kaʻahumanu, at the end of which he publicly fornicated with his sister, who he in fact loved deeply. A marriage between the king and his sister, both chiefs of very high genealogical rank, had been opposed by Kaʻahumanu because any children from the union would possess unchallengeable *mana.* Sahlins notes that the couple's public display was 'the consummate royal gesture, traditionally symbolic of a refusal to share power' (1981: 66; see also Ralston 1985: 321).

Conclusion

For Foucault, the genealogical concept of 'emergence' described a 'series of subjugations' that were the proper object of history (Foucault 1984a: 83). In a 'non-place' of confrontation 'only a single drama is ever staged: the endlessly repeated play of dominations' through which subjects are formed. Humanity, he claimed, 'installs each of its "violences" in a system of rules and thus proceeds from domination to domination' (ibid.: 85). In eastern and central Polynesia new 'violences' were indeed installed in systems of rules – codes of law introduced at seasonally appropriate times. But in this particular place there were also many dramas staged in opposition to these rules. In Tahiti, a court sitting at which a judge became the accused and a dwarf became the judge was one of many seasonal performances that reversed, mocked or ridiculed the new order.

Although it had been seasonally introduced, judicial power knew no seasonality of life. Relentless and active day and night throughout the entire year, this power, as practice, was particularly directed towards the repression of youthful exuberance and bodily display. It is not surprising, therefore, that although often supported by chiefs and high-chiefs, the 'rebellions' were largely reaffirmations of a seasonality of life by a generation that included many emerging leaders.

Any suggestion that the judges should blindfold themselves, heap layers of cloth over themselves or go into hiding at Christmas would have been considered ridiculous by the missionaries. But the judges and missionaries might have allowed Christmas itself to be a time of revelry. Had they done so, Christian conversion might have taken a very different course, accommodating rather than denying a Polynesian seasonality of power.

8

History, *Habitus* and Seasonality

Lined up along the wall at the back of my desk is a series of cardboard boxes I use for filing copies of archival documents. At the outset of this project I adopted two labelling systems: One organized the material into islands and the other, comprising three boxes labelled simply I, II and III, organized the material in terms of Van Gennep's and Turner's three-stage model of the ritual process. I guessed early on that the ritual schema of separation, liminality and reintegration might be loosely expressed in the events I was about to explore and, in any case, I felt it would do as an initial framework for my inquiry.

As it turned out, the Polynesian Iconoclasm and its aftermath did follow this schema in a very loose sense. The destruction of temples and images undoubtedly resulted in a separation of priests, chiefs and the wider population from their gods. The sacrificial exchange between them was terminated by iconoclasm. The subsequent generalized liminality and its associated *communitas* took varying forms. In the Society Islands a rapid construction of small chapels and mass interest in acquiring and learning to read printed texts occurred during a period of relative freedom from hierarchical and priestly controls. In Rarotonga, people gathered in one settlement and worked together to construct a large church of social unity. In Hawai'i there was a five-year interregnum between the iconoclasm and the imposition of a Christian order during which the relative freedoms of the *makahiki* season were extended. Reintegration and the re-imposition of hierarchy everywhere coincided with the construction of new churches and the proclamation of Biblically-justified laws. While churches were not *marae* or *heiau* temples, and laws were not the old tabus, the chiefly hierarchies retained many of their pre-Christian features and were, in some respects, strengthened through centralization.

But in recognizing the applicability of this general model we have not moved very far from my initial understandings. What is missing from the model is the culturally conditioned agency, the ritual praxis, through which the social transformations were produced. Missing are the priest-led improvisations on seasonal practices and the distinctive dispositions that motivated them. Conceptualizing the Polynesian Iconoclasm and its aftermath as rituopraxis required me to abandon Turner in favour of Bourdieu and Sahlins. While, for my purposes, there was too little history in Bourdieu and too little *habitus* in Sahlins, when their theoretical insights were combined they became a powerful lens through which to view history as practice.

In the most general sense, this book is intended to be a contribution to practice history. Practice histories, as Sherry Ortner emphasized in *High Religion,* her own splendid contribution to the genre, combine the concept of practice with disparate notions of structure (1989: 13). Ortner herself combined practice with a notion of structure as 'cultural schemas' – 'plot structures that recur throughout many cultural stories and rituals that depict actors responding to the contradictions of their culture and dealing with them in appropriate, even "heroic" ways' (ibid.: 14). I argued in the Introduction that Sahlins combined practice with structure as both cosmological schemes and popular *habitus.*

The dominant eastern Polynesian schema of seasonality explored in this book existed as both cosmological structure and embodied *habitus.* As cosmology, it was the cyclical movement of gods between worlds of humanity and divinity, a movement indexed by the appearance and disappearance of Pleiades on the evening horizon. As *habitus,* the schema of seasonality was a system of hierarchically differentiated expectations, attitudes and urgencies that guided participation in the ritual practices of political life. Rituopraxis as iconoclasm, church construction and consecration, scriptural printing and distribution, judicial practice and opposition to missionary orders is best conceived, not as the putting of prior cosmological understandings into practice but, instead, as improvisation upon earlier ritual practices guided by *habitus.* While Sahlins stressed relationships between historical practice and *cosmological* precedent, I prioritize relationships between historical practice and *ritual* precedent, improvisation upon the latter being guided by *habitus.*

In emphasizing improvisation, I have sought to reconcile radical change, or rupture, and embodied continuity. Inspired by his fieldwork among the millennial Urapmin of Papua New Guinea, Joel Robbins has challenged anthropologists of Christianity to take more seriously emic understandings of Christian conversion as cultural rupture and to develop models of change that 'comprehend discontinuity but that give us non-trivial insights into how processes and projects of both continuity and discontinuity shape cultural transformation (Robbins 2007: 32; see also Robbins 2003). A disciplinary over-commitment to continuity-thinking, including a search for 'deeper' traditions below Christian 'surfaces' has, he argues, hindered the development of such models. A strong case has been made, I think, for an anthropological approach that does not reduce the rupture of conversion to the continuity of tradition.

I have sought to develop such an approach in this book by drawing on the concepts of rituopraxis, improvisation and *habitus,* concepts that allow us to recognize both rupture and continuity. The conversion of east Polynesia was indeed revolutionary, but it was also revolutionary improvisation. While it is important not to reduce discontinuity to continuity, it is equally important to recognize that structure, including *habitus,* cannot change overnight. The force of *habitus* can certainly have radical, even rupturing effects when it orchestrates rituopraxis, but it can also act as a force of inertia.

In the remainder of this chapter I want to reflect upon the revolutionary changes described in this book and argue that they require us to understand the force of *habitus* as historical in these two distinct senses: Firstly, *habitus is future-oriented.* It differentially shapes historical desire so that particular contingent projects are understood as the most reasonable courses of action in the circumstances, and it guides improvisation through which whole social contexts are transformed in accordance with particular tastes and desires. Secondly, *habitus is past-oriented.* The historicity of *habitus* is also that of inertia, influencing the ways and extent to which people accommodate (and fail to accommodate) changing social contexts, contexts themselves partly products of improvisation guided by *habitus* in its future oriented mode. Bourdieu emphasized only the second of these historical modes in his writings, and so greatly under-estimated the full historical force of *habitus.* In contrast, in the discussion which follows I emphasize the first – historical intention and improvisation – although I will also have something to say about inertia as well.

Habitus and Desire

The concept of *habitus* includes motivational dispositions that give impetus and direction to historical change. Bourdieu originally referred to *habitus* as a 'motor' in a discussion of the way in which a sense of honour served as the motivational disposition for a 'whole dialectic of challenge and riposte, gift and counter-gift' in Mediterranean societies (Bourdieu 1980: 130). I think we might extend this idea to include historical agency more generally: if a disposition to seek, increase and defend honour (*mana* in Polynesia) can be understood to motivate everyday practices of reciprocity, then it might also be understood as a motor for reciprocity writ large, that is, reciprocity as a historical strategy employed in forming alliances between high chiefs and Europeans and between humanity and divinity. In addition to the chiefly disposition to protect and increase *mana,* a variety of other motivational dispositions were also in play for priests and ordinary people during the Polynesian Iconoclasm and its immediate aftermath. In the following discussion I identify some of the more important of these, focusing on regionally-shared differences between the dispositions of high-chiefs, priests and commoners. The course of the regional iconoclasm and its aftermath was, I suggest, partly motivated by a concordance of these dispositions.

Chiefly *mana* was associated, more closely than priestly *mana*, with a disposition to assume precedence and the sense that the chief embodied in his person the social totality that he represented. Sahlins has used the term 'heroic' to label the mode of history for which this disposition was a motor, and we might also reasonably use this term as a name for the disposition itself. The chiefly polities of Polynesia were, Sahlins proposed, 'heroic systems' associated with

> a certain mode of historical production, a kind of historical practice. One aspect of this practice ... is the sense of history as incorporated in the chiefly person and expressed in his current action ... Embodying and making history, ruling chiefs thus practice socially the capacities that they were given cosmologically. (Sahlins 2000: 324–25)

Of course, we might also reverse this and conclude that ruling chiefs (and their priests) elaborated cosmologically the capacities that they were given socially. Sahlins further noted that the chiefly embodiment of totality was reflected in the chiefly use of the first person personal pronoun 'I' to refer to his group, and that heroic histories were characterized by 'an unusual capacity for sudden change or rupture' (1985: 41). This last observation is particularly insightful in light of the events described in this book.

Sahlins has argued persuasively that 'the resources of political power in Austronesian societies and numerous others are generally foreign' (2012: 139). In the early nineteenth century, a chiefly, heroic disposition to totalize society via allegiance to and identification with the British monarch as an outside power was clearly one of the motors for the dramatic transformation of political fields in the Society Islands and Hawai'i. Pomare and Liholiho would embody the new order as 'kings'.

Pomare regarded himself as closely allied to the British monarch. In 1807 he formally presented an entire district of Tahiti to King George. Ellis recorded:

> The king [Pomare] having nearly exterminated his enemies in the larger peninsula and deprived the Taiarabuans of their muskets, the land of the vanquished was distributed among his friends and favourites; large tracts were set apart for the idol Oro, to be occupied only by his priests and some would have been appropriated to the true God had not the missionaries objected. One district, Utu Maoro, was, in the public distribution, given to King George and the men of Britain and confirmed in a written document which the king gave the missionaries. (1844 I: 189)

We have seen that immediately after Pomare's eviction from Tahiti to Mo'orea two years later, a picture of King George that had been sent to Pomare from England was taken by his enemies to Oro's *marae* and offered up as a sacrifice (Davies 1961: 130). The English king, Pomare and their god had, for the time being at least, been encompassed by the local god. In 1817, following his unification of Tahiti, Pomare wrote to the missionaries at Moʻorea expressing his 'determination to visit England' (Orsmond to LMS, 30 June 1817, SSL).

For Pomare and Hawaiian chiefs one of the attractions of Christianity was that it was the religion of the British monarch. Liholiho was quite explicit on this point. In a letter to King George IV in 1823 he wrote: 'The former idolatrous system has been abolished in these islands as we wish the protestant religion of your Majesty's dominions to be practiced here' (translation in Tyerman and Bennet 1841: 127). As Sahlins has noted, Kamehameha I considered King George III to be his 'older brother' and he addressed him so by letter (Sahlins 2012: 143):

> Kamehameha was flying the Union Jack from his house and canoe even before he ceded the Hawaiian Islands to 'King George' and he still considered himself under the British Monarch's protection after the offer had been refused. (Sahlins 2012: 143)

After the death of King George III, eight months after the death of Kamehameha, the latter's son, Liholiho, considered Hawaiʻi to be one of George IV's 'dominions', as did most Hawaiians at the time of the iconoclasm: 'They regard this country as belonging to King George (this idea seems to have taken strong possession of the minds of all classes of native)' (Tyerman and Bennet 1841: 101).

For the ruling chiefs of the Austral Islands and the Cook Islands, meanwhile, the foreign power that served as the most immediate reference point for social totalization was, initially at least, Pomare. Pomare had transformed himself into a 'king' by associating himself with the source of European *mana* and this was good reason, if not reason enough, for his iconoclasm to be emulated.

In contrast to the more heroic disposition of high chiefs, a priestly disposition was more strongly conditioned by identification with gods through a close fellowship with them. The priests fed, wrapped and slept with the gods. A priestly disposition was also strongly conditioned by participation in human social life as a member of a *tapu,* highly-trained elite with a developed taste for discipline, metaphor and abstraction. Writing of the Hawaiian priest as a leading participant in sacrifices, Valeri concluded:

> He is permanently in contact with the god ... and that participating in this way in the god's nature and *mana,* even being his manifestation in human form, he can function as mediator between sacrifier and the god. In the person of the sacrificer, human actions are translated into divine actions, divine actions into human ones. (Valeri 1985: 130–31)

The temple priest (*kahu atua*) assigned to 'feed' a god via daily sacrifices was identified with the god to the extent that he was fed on the god's behalf during the *luakini* rites described in Chapter 1 (Valeri 1985: 135).

This godly identification may have attained its highest expression in Hawai'i, but it was also evident to varying degrees throughout eastern Polynesia. Wilson records, for example, that the Tahitian priest, Hamanemane, was dressed as a god, wrapped in a fantastic, possibly frightening, garment of red and black feathers, and that he spoke as the god on the *marae* (Wilson 1799: 337). Indeed, the Tahitian priest was referred to *as* a god (*atua*) when he performed in this way and, significantly for us, he was later sacrificed as one (Ellis 1829b: 235–37). Ellis records that priests in Huahine slept with their gods in a god-house built atop a high pole. Tane and the lesser gods had keepers who constantly attended them (1829b: 202). A Huahine priest told Ellis that because his god took the form of a shark, he could not be harmed by these animals. Indeed, he added that a shark had once carried him home on its back from the neighbouring island of Ra'iatea (Ellis 1829b: 196). The 'feeding', caring for and dwelling with god-images cultivated and maintained an active fellowship between gods and priests. Thus, in Tahiti, a priest was sometimes termed 'friend of the gods' (*tau atua*) and collectively priests were termed 'the side dwelling with the gods' (*pae tau aitu*) (Henry 1928: 154). This fellowship was also evident in the Southern Cook Islands. We saw in Chapter 1 that a Mangaian priest dwelt with and fed his gods daily. In Rarotonga, also, priests were assigned to care for particular gods (Sissons 2007: 53). Sharing of food and kava with gods during the public feasts that accompanied the *pa'iatua*, *aka'au takurua* and *luakini* rites of hierarchy were also expressions of this sacred fellowship.

It is no accident that priests were so widely associated with sharks. Priests announced sacrifices, foretold of death and were believed to be able to kill through sorcery. Although sorcerers comprised a distinct class of priests in Tahiti and Hawai'i (and possibly in the Southern Cook Islands), where they were outside the official temple hierarchies, all priests were thought capable of sorcery (Valeri 1985: 138; Henry 1928: 166). Moerenhout writes that the Tahitian priests, as godly representatives, were treated with respect by all, even the chiefs. By way of example, he notes that when a priest travelled through a district to announce a *ra'ui* (prohibition) he was fed and feared as a god. Food for him was

> laid out only upon a piece of cloth which had enveloped or touched the images of the gods. Everyone then, even the chiefs, had to lower their faces to the ground at his passing, and no-one would dare to pronounce a single word as long as one heard his cries. (1983: 241)

The formal inculcation of a priestly disposition took place during a period of strict religious training for boys who had usually been selected from priestly or chiefly families; priestly titles were generally hereditary (Tyerman and Bennet 1841: 137; Maretu 1983: 44, 88; Ellis 1829b: 208; Henry 1928: 154; Moerenhout 1983: 239). This training included an instilling of attitudes required for living in fellowship with gods: avoidance of impurity, correctness (*tika/tia*) in behaviour and speech, especially concerning things deemed to be *tapu*. This disciplined attitude reflected the nature of the knowledge imparted during training – *tapu*, abstract and cosmologically totalizing – and in the faultless memorization required of trainees.

Priests in the Society Islands were taught astronomy, regional geography and the navigational knowledge to which they were both linked. A famous map drawn by the priest Tupaia for Captain Cook, showing the Society Islands, the Austral Islands and some of the Tuamotu Islands, is good evidence of such a regional knowledge. They learned mythology, genealogy, heraldry and the calculation of the seasons. Prayers were memorized for calling the gods into images, success in war, binding prisoners, sorcery and many other purposes. Priests were also taught the arts of statesmanship: public speech-making; rhetoric, including the use of metaphor and simile; and how to sue for peace (Henry 1928: 154–55; Tyerman and Bennet 1841: 88). Elsewhere across eastern Polynesia, novice priests received similar training and in the Southern Cook Islands this included being taught traditions that linked their islands to Ra'iatea and Tahiti (Maretu 1983: 189; Williams 1839: 56–57, 104).

The *tapu* nature of the knowledge imparted during priestly training and the emphasis on accurate memorization did not mean, of course, that innovation was precluded. Ritual innovation characterized 'conversions' to 'Oro, for example, as the Ra'iatean priesthood extended its influence outwards from Ra'iatea throughout the Society Islands in the second half of the eighteenth century. The god, Hiro, was also apparently growing in influence at this time; Auna, Ellis's friend who recorded the destruction of Hawai'i's god-images in 1822, was one of Hiro's priests. He informed the visiting LMS delegation to Huahine in 1822 that 'Hiro, the patron divinity of thieves was devoutly worshipped here and throughout the islands, though he was a god of but recent creation. He is said to have been a native of Ra'iatea' (Tyerman and Bennet 1841: 68). A readiness to include elements of Western power into Tahitian cosmology is evident in Captain Wilson's description of a priestly oration that accompanied the transfer of land to the LMS mission in 1797. The priest, Hamanemane, named all the *atua*, districts and chiefs in order, and then concluded with a list of ships and their commanders, beginning with Wallis, Bougainville and Cook (Wilson 1799: 76).

Polynesian priests had strongly developed tastes for other-worldly knowledge about such matters as geography, health and new construction techniques. The Europeanizing projects of high-chiefs promised greater access to this. More significantly, literacy gave access to the wealth of sacred knowledge contained in the Bible and elsewhere. But because this literacy and knowledge was, potentially, available to all, priests needed to take a lead if they were to retain their *mana*. We will probably never know the particular reasons why Pati'i or Hewahewa chose to participate in the centralizing projects of their respective high-chiefs (and, indeed, historians have wondered why Hewahewa in particular freely gave up his power). But threats to *mana* associated with the declining value of their ritual expertise were probably a significant motivation in these and other cases.

The notion of *habitus* and the associated concept of improvisation enable us to steer a course between overly voluntarist history that privileges the intentionality of agents, and an overly objective history that attributes agency to structures and institutions rather than to the conditioned subjectivity of actors. When Society Islands priests engaged with LMS missionaries, they did so as institutions made flesh, bringing to their interactions motivational dispositions more or less adjusted to the institutional contexts in which they were formed. Despite many profound differences, these priests and missionaries shared institutionally conditioned tastes for discipline, respect, correctness, control, ritual leadership, metaphor and abstract totalization. Both sets of historical actors were predisposed to become law-makers and judges. The transformation of seasonal, sacrificial societies into Christian ones was guided, then, by a partial concordance of priestly and missionary dispositions: the motivational dispositions of Polynesian priests and missionaries were 'roughly attuned', as Bourdieu put it, enough so to allow collusion in church construction, print-centralization and judicial practices (2000: 145). Indeed, Bourdieu termed such concordance '*collusio*'.

The rituopraxis of large church construction is an excellent example of such *collusio*. Initially, this 'consecrated industry' (as Handy termed it) was directed by chiefs and former priests, some of whom were specialists in this work. However, as their influence increased, European missionaries became more involved in design and construction. Churches were, in other words, materializations of the *collusio* of missionaries, priest and chiefs. The buildings had different significance for each set of actors, but they were nonetheless the product of motivating dispositions that were roughly attuned. It was a similar case for the laws drawn up by chiefs with the assistance of missionaries and adopted at the mass openings of churches during the season of Pleiades below. These, too, were products of *collusio*.

The concept of *collusio* nicely complements Sahlins's 'structure of the conjuncture': while the 'structure of the conjuncture' highlights different understandings inherent in cross-cultural engagements such as those between priests and missionaries, *collusio* focuses our attention upon the shared understandings that are grounded in a partial concordance of dispositions. Sahlins's notion of the 'structure of the conjuncture' understands practices of cross-cultural engagement as having 'their own dynamics' that do not directly follow from cultural expectations. Instead, the limits and pragmatics of practice take over and bring about a revision in cultural expectations and ultimately conceptual schemes (1981: 35, 38). *Collusio* understands practices of cross-cultural engagement as made possible by partially-shared expectations, urgencies and attitudes, these guided by dispositions that are roughly attuned to each other. Practice history requires both concepts.

In contrast to the *tapu/kapu* existence of high-chiefs and priests, especially the latter's disciplined, correct disposition, the lives of common people were *noa*, that is, relatively free. A popular disposition to avoid life-threatening *tapu/kapu* and assert the life-enhancing freedom of *noa* was embodied and reproduced in practices of seasonality. Popular support for the iconoclastic and post-iconoclastic actions of priests and chiefs through participation in seasonally appropriate transgressions of *tapu/kapu* was, in part, motivated by such a *noa* disposition.

In addition to a popular *habitus* of *tapu*-avoidance and seasonally-timed transgression, a common disposition to honour chiefs through generosity was also in play in the aftermath of the iconoclasms. The labour that was contributed by many ordinary people to the construction of large churches honoured chiefs and high-chiefs in the same way that the construction of temples and chiefs' houses had previously. Giving in this way, like the offering of food, mats and canoes, was an expression of love and respect (known in different Polynesian languages by the terms *aloha, aroha,* or *aroʻa*) for chiefs.

Interestingly, prior to the Polynesian Iconoclasm, all of the motivational dispositions that we have been considering here had been brought into play during the first engagements between Hawaiians and Captain Cook. Sahlins highlighted the centrality of the sacrificial schema in his account, noting:

> The Hawaiians had at first conceived their practical transactions with Captain Cook on the model of sacrifice. Their initial gifts were small pigs, presented as offerings together with banana plants, sugar cane and ritual formulas suitable on such occasions. Priests took the lead in these prestations. (1981: 37)

Sahlins went on to explain that chiefs and commoners acted differently in accordance with their respective dispositions. Chiefs exchanged goods of high *mana* and asserted their precedence, while commoner women offered their sexuality to Cook's men, following the practice termed *ʻimi haku,* expressing *aloha* in order to cultivate chiefly and divine connections (ibid.: 40).

Habitus and Inertia

The sacrificial regeneration of pre-Christian Polynesian societies followed a temporal logic of practice tied to the appearance and disappearance of Pleiades on the evening horizon. But this renewal can also be understood as part of a seasonal exchange between humanity and gods, mediated by priests. In his anthropologically famous critique of structuralists' understandings of the gift and their failure to grasp its practical logic, Bourdieu argued that a return gift has to be deferred and different from its earlier precursor, if it is to appear as an act of generosity, that is as a gift (1980: 105; 2000: 191–92). This means that the temporal gap, integral to the nature of the gift, is always open to strategic manipulation.

Similarly, the divine return for sacrifice, as a gift, also has to be understood as different from the offering and delayed if it is to appear as an act of generosity. Indeed, it is only because it is both delayed and unpredictable that the return for sacrifice appears as an act of specifically *divine* generosity. Unpredictability is, as Bourdieu pointed out, a characteristic of absolute power, human, and by extension, divine:

> Absolute power is the power to make oneself unpredictable and deny other people any reasonable anticipation, to place them in total uncertainty by offering no scope to their capacity to predict. This power, an extreme that is never reached *except in the theological imagination,* with the unjust omnipotence of a wicked god, frees its possessor from the experience of time as powerlessness. The all-powerful is he who does not wait but who makes others wait ... *waiting implies submission.* (Bourdieu 2000: 228, emphasis added)

In calling forth and dismissing gods to the rhythm of Pleiades, thus effecting a passage from *communitas* to hierarchy and vice versa, priests were appropriating divine power by rendering its unpredictability seasonally predictable. This is represented in Figure 8.1.

As shown in the diagram, offerings to gods via the priest (A) occurred during rites of hierarchy when Pleiades dipped below the horizon. These ensured the return of the gods and with them fertility and future life (B) that occurred in association with rites of *communitas*. While the size of the divine return remained unknown its timing was now more predictable and with this predictability a degree of power (*mana*) had been transferred from gods to priests. The power of gods in Polynesia was, then, less than absolute. The predictable, priest-assisted re-appearance of the gods (or god, in the case of Lono) during the rites of *communitas* meant that *mana* was shared, albeit still unequally, between priests and gods who entered into a kind of fellowship.

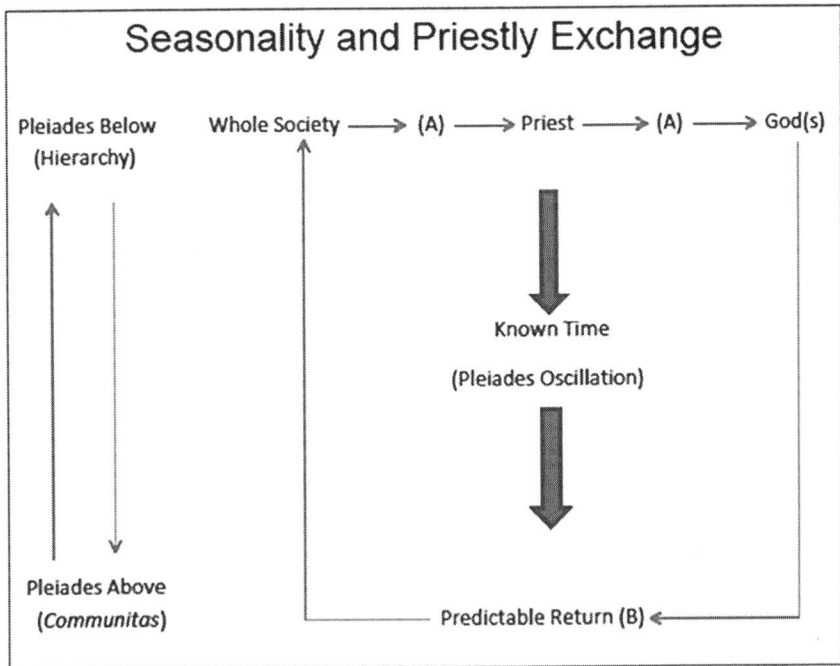

Figure 8.1. Diagram of seasonality and priestly exchange.

When we understand the centrality of this annual temporal schema it becomes clear why the notion of Christian conversion as a mere substitution of one god for many is so misleading. What was involved here is much more than a substitution of Jehova for pre-Christian *atua*; it is the abandonment of an entire ritual temporality from which a great deal of priestly power had been derived. Priests could only remain at the centre of ritual life by abandoning a privileged fellowship with the divine that had been founded on seasonality and submitting to the unpredictable generosity of a new god possessing absolute power.

But we should also note that the practical schema represented by the diagram endured for some time after the abandonment of priestly predictability. Offerings (labelled 'A' in Figure 8.1) took the form of god-images during episodes of iconoclasm, and then the giving of building materials and collective labour for church construction in the aftermath of these iconoclastic episodes. While the 'Return' (labelled 'B' in Figure 8.1) became unpredictable, a preliminary form it took was the provisioning of spelling books and religious texts that embodied the life-giving word of Jehova. Indeed, on Aitutaki images were directly exchanged for spelling books, an exchange mediated by the Christian 'priests' from Ra'iatea.

The dissolution of a close fellowship between priests and gods maintained through practices of seasonality also meant that priestly *habitus* would now come under enormous pressure to change. The initial obdurate resistance by some priests to the introduction of Christianity was no doubt founded on a recognition that, in addition to a loss of *mana*, a transformation of self would be required by this change of religion. For some, a loss of power would also be a bodily change. The LMS delegation recorded, for example, that a priest in Huahine had become blind, the sudden affliction possibly reflecting his inability to reconcile his old *habitus* with the new order:

> But what gave peculiar interest to his person and character was the circumstance of his being blind, the occasion of his blindness and its effect on his future life. The dark idolater had long withstood the gospel and refused to acknowledge the sanctity of the Sabbath after the former was received and the latter commanded by authority to be observed in these islands. One Sabbath morning, in contempt of the day, he went out to work in his garden. On returning to his house he became blind in a moment. (Tyerman and Bennet 1841: 64)

As I noted earlier, Bourdieu's understanding of *habitus* as history emphasized the historical adjustment and non-adjustment of *habitus* to changing social contexts or fields:

> Moreover, even if dispositions may waste away or weaken through lack of use (linked, in particular, to a change in social position or condition), or as a result of heightened consciousness associated with an effort of transformation (such as the correction of accents, manners etc.), there is an inertia (or *hysteresis*) of *habitus* which have a spontaneous tendency (based in biology) to perpetuate structures corresponding to their conditions of production. As a result, it can happen that, in what might be called the Don Quixote effect, dispositions are out of line with the field and with 'collective expectations' which are constitutive of its normality. This is the case, in particular, when a field undergoes a major crisis and its regularities (even its rules) are profoundly changed. (Bourdieu 2000: 160)

Bourdieu went on to note that even under normal circumstances *habitus* is often confronted with conditions different from those in which it was produced – in which cases people may 'lose touch' and perpetuate dispositions appropriate to an earlier era or consciously work to retrain, with varying degrees of success, their dispositions as they move into new situations and confront new experiences. This latter process of an almost permanent revision of dispositions, which is never radical, can be contrasted with changes to *habitus* in situations of crisis, including those associated with colonialism. In these situations, Bourdieu speculated,

> agents often have difficulty in holding together the dispositions associated with different states or stages, and some of them, often those who were best adapted to the previous state of the game, have difficulty adjusting to the new established order. Their dispositions become dysfunctional and the efforts they make to perpetuate them help to plunge them deeper into failure. (Bourdieu 2000: 161–62)

However, while instances of dysfunctional dispositions and an inability to adjust dispositions to new Christian social contexts can certainly be found in the missionary record, as perhaps in the case of the priest who suddenly went blind, they are not as common as Bourdieu's armchair theorizing would lead us to assume. High-priests and high-chiefs – those 'best adapted to the previous state of the game' – were often the most successful in the new 'game'. More significant, I think, were the more generalized pressures that were brought to bear on the populations at large. In Polynesia the new ritual contexts that included weekly ritual cycles of mass worship contradicted a *habitus* more closely adjusted to the seasonality of life. As a direct result of profound changes in the extent and nature of popular participation in ritual life, ordinary people became more priestly and priests became more ordinary. Practical changes in ritual life were supported by re-materializations of ritual fields, such as most dramatically the replacement of temples, from which ordinary men and women were generally excluded, with temples within which whole populations were ideally included as participants in the same ritual events.

Priests no longer had an exclusive fellowship with the divine, but rather this fellowship became ideally available to and cultivated by all people. Where formerly only priests and chiefs embodied divinity, now everybody might be filled with the Holy Spirit. Ritual communication with the divine through prayer and chanting became a skill available to all who had learned to read and had memorized scripture. Exclusive priestly relationships with god-images were replaced by popular relationships with texts. All now had potential access to sacred knowledge and actively participated in weekly ritual cycles, including domestic prayers. The sorcery of priests was less feared because Christian prayer and piety brought Jehova's protection. Of course, where former priests had compensated for their loss of power by assuming senior positions within the church hierarchy or judiciary, earlier attitudes of fear and respect towards them remained. Priestly anxieties over bodily control shifted from food to sexuality, but the focus remained on ritual purity: the whole body had to be covered in church, for example.

In the new rituo-practical production of Christian societies, the certainties of priest-controlled seasonality gave way to foreign sickness, hope and uncertainty over whether Jehova would provide abundance and new life. Within a few years this uncertainty began to contribute to a growing sense, felt by many ordinary people, particularly the youth, of missionary and chiefly oppression. For many people their new 'priestliness' was experienced as an oppressive excess of *tapu*. This was resisted in bodily ways, that is, with expressions of *habitus* that were entirely appropriate to the former seasonality: sexual freedom, extravagant sartorial adornment, tattooing and sports. Thus old *communitas* was asserted in opposition to the new hierarchy and the ritual pressures it imposed, reflecting the fact that people's *habitus* was not yet in full in accord with the new ritual orders of Protestantism.

In the Introduction to this book I proposed that the relationship between history and *habitus* is dialectical. On the one hand, history is practically improvised, differently so in different societies. On the other hand, the historical results of this improvisation transform *habitus*. While Bourdieu noted this dialectic, his understanding of it was one-sided. He emphasized the role of *habitus* as a conservative force. The Polynesian Iconoclasm demonstrates, however, that *habitus* acts equally forcefully in its future-oriented mode. If I have emphasized the latter in this book, then I, too, must plead guilty to a charge of one-sidedness. But it has been unavoidable in my case. Detailed consideration of the conservatism of priestly, chiefly and popular *habitus* reflected in the many adjustments and failed adjustments to Christian life in the aftermath of the Polynesian Iconoclasm would require a much longer time frame than the one employed here. The longer-term processes that would need to be examined would include ones of pious self-transformation, gendered social repression, bodily discipline and transformations of *mana*. But such important further topics will have to wait for a future practice history.

Documented seasonal events referred to in the text				
	Pleiades below (hierarchy) (May to July)		Pleiades above (communitas) (November to January)	
Year	Islands	Events	Islands	Events
1815	Mo'orea Tahiti	*Pa'iatua* rejected via *marae*/image destruction Feathers of images desecrated	Tahiti Ra'iatea Huahine	*Marae*/image destruction (Nov 1815 to Jan 1816)
1816			Maupiti	*Marae*/image destruction
1817	Tahiti Mo'orea	Work on 'Royal Chapel' Printing press consecrated		
1818	Mo'orea	Large church opened		
1819	Tahiti	'Royal Chapel' opened	Hawai'i	*Heiau*/image destruction
1820	Ra'iatea Huahine Hawai'i	Large church opened (April) Large church opened Kaua'i church built	Ra'ivavae	*Marae* destruction and image desecration
1821			Tubuai Rimatara	*Marae* destruction and image desecration
1822	Mo'orea Aitutaki	Octagonal church opened High chief rejects *pa'iatua*	Ra'iatea Aitutaki	Tea drinking festivities *Marae* destruction

1823	Mauke and Mitiaro Hawai'i	Churches built to replace *marae* Large churches built by chiefs	Tahiti Rarotonga	Mock court-sitting/ revelry *Marae*/image destruction begin
1824	Rarotonga	First large church built		
1826	Hawai'i	Preaching circuits by Ka'ahumanu begin		
1827	Rarotonga	Large Takitumu church built	Hawai'i	Revelry
1829	Hawai'i	Large Honolulu church opened		
1831			Rarotonga	Revelry
1832			Hawai'i	Revelry
1833			Hawai'i	Revelry

References

Auna. n.d. 'Extracts from the Journal of Auna (native teacher) during a voyage to Hawaii May 11–July 2'. SSL.

Babadzan, A. 1993. *Les Dépouilles des Dieux: Essai sur la Religion Tahititienne à l'époque de la Découverte,* Paris: Fondation de la Maison des Sciences de l'Homme.

——. 2003. 'The Gods Stripped Bare'. In *Clothing the Pacific,* edited by C. Colchester, 25–50. Oxford and New York: Berg.

Barratt, G. 1992. *The Tuamotu Islands and Tahiti.* Volume 4 of *Russia and the South Pacific, 1696–1840.* Vancouver: UBC Press.

Beechy, Capt. F. 1832. *Narrative of a Voyage to the Pacific and Beerings Strait.* Philadelphia: Carey and Lea.

Best, E. 2005 [1924]. *Maori Religion and Mythology: Being an Account of Cosmogeny, Anthopogeny, Religious Beliefs and Rites, Magic and Folk Lore of the Maori Folk of New Zealand.* 2 vols. Wellington: Te Papa Press.

——. 1972. *Tuhoe, the Children of the Mist.* Vol. 1. Wellington: A. H. and A. W. Reed.

Bingham, H. 1981. *A Residence of Twenty-one Years in the Sandwich Islands.* Rutland, Vermont and Tokyo: Charles E. Tuttle Co.

Bishop, A. 1827. Letter. *Missionary Herald* 23: 247.

Bloch, M. 1992. *Prey into Hunter: The Politics of Religious Experience.* Cambridge: Cambridge University Press.

Bourdieu, P. 1977. *Outline of a Theory of Practice.* Cambridge: Cambridge University Press.

——. 1980. *The Logic of Practice.* Translated by R. Nice. Stanford, CA: Stanford University Press.

——. 2000. *Pascalian Meditations.* Translated by R. Nice. Stanford, CA: Stanford University Press.

——. 2008. *The Bachelor's Ball: The Crisis of Peasant Society in Bearn.* Translated by R. Nice. Cambridge: Polity Press.

Bourne, R. n.d. 'Journal of a Voyage to the Harvey-Islands [*sic*] etc.' *Quarterly Chronicle* III: 261–67.

Bourne, R., and J. Williams. n.d. 'Voyage to the Hervey Islands'. SSJ, Box 5.

Broeze, J. 1988. *A Merchant's Perspective: Captain Jacobus Boelen's Narrative of his Visit to Hawai'i in 1828.* Honolulu: The Hawaiian Historical Society.

Buck, Sir P. 1934. *Mangaian Socety, B.P. Bishop Museum Bulletin* 122. Honolulu: Bishop Museum.

——. 1993. *Mangaia and the Mission.* Edited and with an introduction by R. Dixon and T. Parima. Suva: Institute of Pacific Studies.

Campbell, A. 1967 [1822]. *A Voyage Round the World from 1806 to 1812.* Facsimile ed. Honolulu: University of Hawaii Press.

Cressy, 1986. 'Books as Totems in Seventeenth-Century England and New England'. *The Journal of Library History* 21, no. 1: 92–106.

Crowl, L. 2008. "Politics and Book Publishing in the Pacific Islands." PhD diss., University of Woolongong.

D'Alleva, A. 2001. 'Captivation, Representation and the Limits of Cognition: Interpreting Metaphor and Metonymy in Tahitian Taumau'. In *Beyond Aesthetics: Art and Technologies of Enchantment,* edited by C. Pinney and N. Thomas, 79–96. Oxford: Berg.

Daley, M. 2008. 'Another Agency in His Great Work: The Beginnings of Missionary Printing in Tonga'. *Journal of Pacific History* 43, no. 3: 367–74.

Davenport, W. 1969. '"The Hawaiian Cultural Revolution": Some Political and Economic Considerations'. *American Anthropologist* 71:1–20.

Davies, J. 1851. *A Tahitian and English Dictionary.* New York: AMS Press.

———. 1961. *The History of the Tahitian Mission 1799–1830.* Edited by C. Newbury. Cambridge: Cambridge University Press for The Hakluyt Society.

Dibble, S. 1843. *History of the Sandwich Islands.* Lahainaluna, HI: Press of the Mission Seminary.

Eliade, M. 1965. *The Myth of the Eternal Return: Or, Cosmos and History.* Translated by W. Trask. Princeton: Princeton University Press.

Ellen, R. 1988. 'Fetishism'. *Man* (NS) 23, no. 2: 213–35.

Ellis, W. 1828. *Narrative of a Tour through Hawaii or Owhyee, with Remarks on the History, Traditions, Manners, Customs and Language of the Inhabitants of the Sandwich Islands.* London: Fisher, Son and Jackson.

———. 1829a. *Polynesian Researches during a Residence of Nearly Six Years in the South Sea Islands.* Vol. 1. London: Fisher, Son and Jackson.

———. 1829b. *Polynesian Researches during a Residence of Nearly Six Years in the South Sea Islands.* Vol. 2. London: Fisher, Son and Jackson.

———. 1831. *Polynesian Researches during a Residence of Nearly Eight Years in the Society and Sandwich Islands.* 2d ed., vol. 4. London: Fisher, Son and Jackson.

———. 1832. *Polynesian Researches during a Residence of Nearly Eight Years in the Society and Sandwich Islands.* 2d ed., vol. 3. London: Fisher, Son and Jackson.

———. 1834. *Polynesian Researches During a Residence of Nearly Eight Years in the Society and Sandwich Islands.* 2d ed., vol. 2. London: Fisher, Son and Jackson.

———. 1844. *The History of the London Missionary Society.* Vol. 1. London: John Snow.

Foucault, M. 1984a. 'Truth and Power'. Interview with Alessandro Fontana and Pasquale Pasquino. In *The Foucault Reader: An Introduction to Foucault's Thought with Major New Unpublished Material,* edited by P. Rabinow, 51–75. Harmondsworth, U.K.: Penguin.

———. 1984b. 'On the Genealogy of Ethics'. Interview with Paul Rabinow and Hubert Dreyfus. In *The Foucault Reader: An Introduction to Foucault's Thought with Major New Unpublished Material,* edited by P. Rabinow, 340–80. Harmondsworth, U.K.: Penguin.

Gell, A. 1993. *Wrapping in Images: Tattooing in Polynesia.* Oxford: Clarendon Press.

———. 1998. *Art and Agency: An Anthropological Theory.* Oxford: Clarendon Press.

Gill, W. 1846. 'Rarotonga: Opening of a New Chapel at Arorangi', *Missionary Magazine and Chronicle* CXXII July: 102.

———. 1856. *Gems from the Coral Islands: Or Incidents of Contrast Between Savage and Christian Life of the South Sea Islanders.* London: Ward and Co.

———. 1871. *Gems from the Coral Islands: Or Incidents of Contrast between Savage and Christian Life in [sic] the South Sea Islanders.* London: Elliot Stock.

Gill, W. W. 1876. *Myths and Songs from the South Pacific.* London: Henry S. Key.

———. 1894. *From Darkness to Light in Polynesia with Illustrative Clan Songs*. Suva: Institute of Pacific Studies.

Graeber, D. 2005. 'Fetishism as Social Creativity: or, Fetishes are Gods in the Process of Construction'. *Anthropological Theory* 5, no. 4: 407–38.

Griffin, J. 1827. *Memoirs of Capt. James Wilson*. Portland, OR: James Adams.

Gunson, N. 1962. 'An Account of the Mamaia or Visionary Heresy of Tahiti, 1826–1841'. *Journal of the Polynesian Society* 71, no. 2: 209–43.

———. 1966. 'Journal of a Visit to Raivavae in October 1819: by Pomare II, King of Tahiti'. *Journal of Pacific History* 1: 199–203.

———. 1969. 'Pomare II of Tahiti and Polynesian Imperialism'. *Journal of Pacific History* 4:65–82.

Handy, E. 1927. *Polynesian Religion*. Bernice P. Bishop Museum Bulletin 34. Honolulu: Bishop Museum.

———. 1930. *History and Culture in the Society Islands*. Bernice P. Bishop Museum Bulletin 79. Honolulu: Bishop Museum.

———. 1931. *Cultural Revolution in Hawaii*. American Council, Institute of Pacific Relations.

Henry, F. 1995. "The Metaphysics of Militarism: Warfare and Sacrifice as Cosmogonic Practice in Ancient Mangaia". MA diss., University of Chicago.

Henry, T. 1928. *Ancient Tahiti*. Bernice P Bishop Museum Bulletin 48. Honolulu: The Bishop Museum.

Hocart, A. 1933. *The Progress of Man*. London: Methuen.

———. 1934. 'Sacrifice'. In *Encyclopaedia of the Social Sciences* 13, edited by R. Seligman, 501–3. New York: MacMillan.

———. 1954. *Social Origins*. London: Watts.

———. 1970. *Kings and Councillors: An Essay in the Comparative Anatomy of Human Society*. Chicago: University of Chicago Press.

Hooper, S. 2006. *Pacific Encounters: Art and Divinity in Polynesia 1760–1860*. Wellington, NZ: Te Papa Press.

———. 2007. 'Embodying Divinity: The Life of A'a'. *Journal of the Polynesian Society* 116, no. 2: 131–80.

Hubert, H., and M. Mauss. 1964. *Sacrifice: Its Nature and Function*. Translated by W. Halls. London: Cohen and West.

Kaeppler, A. 2007. 'Containers of Divinity'. *Journal of the Polynesian Society* 116, no. 2: 97–130.

Kalakaua, D. 1972. *The Legends and Myths of Hawaii: The Fables and Folklore of a Strange People*. Rutland: Tuttle.

Kamakau, S. M. 1961. *Ruling Chiefs of Hawaii*. Honolulu: Kamehameha Schools Press.

Kirch, P., and R. Green 2001. *Hawaiki, Ancestral Polynesia: An Essay in Historical Anthropology*. Cambridge: Cambridge University Press.

Kroeber, A. 1948. *Anthropology*. Rev. ed. New York: Harcourt Brace and World.

Kuykendall, R. 1938. *The Hawaiian Kingdom: 1778–1854*. Honolulu: University of Hawaii Press.

Lambek, M. 2007. 'Sacrifice and the Problem of Beginning: Meditations from Sakalava Mythopraxis'. *Journal of the Royal Anthropological Institute* (N.S.) 13:19–38.

Levin, S. 1968. 'Overthrow of the *Kapu* System in Hawaii'. *Journal of the Polynesian Society* 77:402–31.

Lingenfelter, R. 1967. *Presses of the Pacific Islands, 1817–1867*. Los Angeles: The Plantin Press.

Linnekin, J. 1990. *Sacred Queens and Women of Consequence: Rank, Gender and Colonialism in the Hawaiian Islands.* Ann Arbor: University of Michigan Press.

London Missionary Society. 1834. *Missionary Voyages among the South Sea Islands.* Boston: Clapp and Broaders.

Malo, D. 1951. *Hawaiian Antiquities.* Translated by N. Emerson. Bernice P. Bishop Museum Special Publication No. 2.

Maretu. 1983. *Cannibals and Converts: Radical Change in the Cook Islands.* Edited and translated by M. Crocombe. Suva: Institute of Pacific Studies.

Missionary Society. n.d. *Missionary Records: Tahiti and Society Islands.* London: Religious Tract Society.

———. 1806. *Transactions of the Missionary Society in the years 1803, 1804, 1805 and 1806.* 3 vols. London: Williams and Smith.

Moerenhout, J. 1983. *Travels to the Islands of the Pacific Ocean.* Translated by A. Borden Jr. Boston: University Press of America.

Mykkanen, J. 2003. *Inventing Politics: A New Political Anthropology of the Hawaiian Kingdom.* Honolulu: University of Hawaii Press.

Newbury, C. 1980. *Tahiti Nui: Change and Survival in French Polynesia 1767–1945.* Honolulu: University of Hawaii Press.

———. 2009. 'Pacts Alliances and Patronage'. *Journal of Pacific History* 44, no. 2: 141–62.

Olaveson, T. 2001. 'Collective Effervescence and Communitas: Processual Models of Ritual and Society in Emile Durkheim and Victor Turner'. *Dialectical Anthropology* 26:89–124.

Oliver, D. 1974. *Ancient Tahitian Society.* 3 vols. Honolulu: University of Hawaii Press.

Orme, W. 1827. *A Defence of the Missions in the South Sea and Sandwich Islands.* London: B. J. Holdsworth.

Ortner, S. 1984. 'Theory in Anthropology since the Sixties'. *Comparative Studies in Society and History* 26, no. 1: 126–66.

———. 1989. *High Religion: A Cultural and Political History of Sherpa Buddhism.* Princeton: Princeton University Press.

Pitman, Charles. 1827–1842. Journal (6 vols). Sydney: State Library of New South Wales.

Prout, E. 1846. *Memoirs of the Life of the Rev. John Williams.* London: John Snow.

Quarterly Review. 1830. Vol. 53. London: John Murray.

Ralston, C. 1985. 'Early Nineteenth Century Millennial Cults and the Case of Hawai'i. *Journal of the Polynesian Society* 94, no. 4: 307–31.

Reilly, M. 2003. *War and Succession in Mangaia from Mamae's Texts.* Auckland: The Polynesian Society.

Robbins, J. 2003. 'On the Paradoxes of Global Pentecostalism and the Perils of Continuity Thinking'. *Religion* 33:221–31.

———. 2007. 'Continuity Thinking and the Problem of Christian Culture: Belief, Time and the Anthropology of Christianity'. *Current Anthropology* 48, no. 1: 5–38.

Rodwell, G. and J. Ramsland, 1999. 'The Maritime Adventures of Joseph Barden [Barsden], According to his own Account, 1799–1816'. *The Great Circle* 21, no. 1: 16–45.

Rodwell, G., ed. 2005. *An Early Colonial Hero: The Amazing Adventures of Josphus Henry Barsden: The Barsden Journal, 1799–1873.* Newcastle, NSW: William Michael Press.

Sahlins, M. 1981. *Historical Metaphors and Mythical Realities: Structure in the Early History of the Sandwich Islands Kingdom.* ASAO Special Publications No. 1. Ann Arbor: University of Michigan Press.

———. 1983. 'Raw Women, Cooked Men and Other "Great Things of the Fiji Islands"'. In *The Ethnography of Cannibalism*, edited by P. Brown and D. Tuzin, 72–93. Washington, DC: Society for Psychological Anthropology.

———. 1985. *Islands of History*. Chicago: University of Chicago Press.

———. 1989. 'Captain Cook at Hawaii'. *Journal of the Polynesian Society* 98, no. 4: 371–423.

———. 1992. *Anahulu: The Anthropology of History in the Kingdom of Hawaii*. Vol. 1. Chicago: University of Chicago Press.

———. 2000. *Culture in Practice: Selected Essays*. New York: Zone Books.

———. 2002. *Waiting for Foucault, Still*. Chicago: Prickly Paradigm Press.

———. 2004. *Apologies to Thucydides: Understanding History as Culture and Vice Versa*. Chicago and London: University of Chicago Press.

———. 2012. 'Alterity and Autochthony: Austronesian Cosmographies of the Marvellous'. *Hau: Journal of Ethnographic Theory* 2, no. 1: 131–60.

Sahlins, M., and D. Barriere. 1979. 'Tahitians in the Early History of Hawaiian Christianity: The Journal of Toketa'. *Hawaiian Journal of History* 13:19–35.

Schutz, A. 1994. *The Voices of Eden: A History of Hawaiian Language Studies*. Honolulu: University of Hawaii Press.

Siikala, J. 1982. *Cult and Conflict in Tropical Polynesia: A Study of Traditional Religion, Christianity and Nativistic Movements*. Helsinki: Academia Scientiarum Fennica.

———. 1991. *Akatokamanava: Myth History and Society in the Southern Cook Islands*. Auckland: The Polynesian Society.

Sissons, J. 1989. 'The Seasonality of Power: The Rarotongan Legend of Tangiia'. *Journal of the Polynesian Society* 98, no. 3: 331–47.

———. 1999. *Nation and Destination: The Creation of Cook Islands Identity*. Suva and Rarotonga: USP Press.

———. 2007. 'From Post to Pillar: God-houses and Social Fields in 19th Century Rarotonga'. *Journal of Material Culture* 12, no. 1: 47–63:

———. 2008. 'Heroic History and Chiefly Chapels in 19th Century Tahiti'. *Oceania* 78, no. 3: 320–31.

———. 2011a. 'The Tectonics of Power: The Hawaiian Iconoclasm and its Aftermath'. *Oceania* 81, no. 2: 205–16.

———. 2011b. 'Sacrifice as History: The Polynesian Iconoclasm'. *Oceania* 81, no. 3: 302–15.

———. 2011c. 'Anthropological Misunderstandings of Hapuu and the Improvisation of Social Life'. *Journal of the Royal Anthropological Institute* (N.S.) 17, no. 3: 628–31.

Smith, W. R. 1894. *Lectures on the Religion of the Semites*. 2d ed. London: A. and C. Black.

Spolsky, E. 2009. 'Literacy after Iconoclasm in the English Reformation'. *Journal of Medieval and Early Modern Studies* 39, no. 2: 305–30.

Stewart, C. 1970 [1830]. *Journal of a Residence in the Sandwich Islands During the Years 1823, 1824, and 1825*. Honolulu: University of Hawaii Press.

Tcherkezoff, S. 2003. 'On Cloth, Gifts and Nudity'. In *Clothing the Pacific*, edited by C. Colchester, 51–75. Oxford and New York: Berg.

Te Ariki-tara-are. 1921. 'History and Traditions of Rarotonga, Part XIX'. *Journal of the Polynesian Society* 30:129–41.

Thomas, N. 1990. *Marquesan Societies: Inequality and Political Transformation in Eastern Polynesia*. Oxford: Clarendon Press.

———. 2003. 'The Case of the Misplaced Ponchos: Speculation Concerning the History of Cloth in Polynesia'. In *Clothing the Pacific,* edited by C. Colchester, 79–96. Oxford and New York: Berg.

Threlkeld, L., and H. Williams to LMS, 8 Oct 1822. 'An Account of the Renunciation of Idolatry and the Reception of Christianity by the Natives of Rururu'. SSL.

Turner, V. 1968. *Drums of Affliction: A Study of Religious Processes among the Ndembu of Zambia.* Oxford: Clarendon Press.

———. 1969. *The Ritual Process: Structure and Anti-structure.* Chicago: Aldine.

———. 1977. 'Sacrifice as Quintessential Process Prophylaxis or Abandonment?' *History of Religions* 16, no. 3: 189–215.

Tyerman, D., and G. Bennet. 1841. *Voyages and Travels Round the World.* Compiled by J. Montgomery. London: John Snow.

Tylor, E. 1874. *Primitive Culture: Researches in the Development of Mythology, Religion, Language, Arts and Custom.* New York: Henry Holt and Co.

Valeri, V. 1985. *Kingship and Sacrifice: Ritual and Society in Ancient Hawaii.* Chicago: University of Chicago Press.

Webb, M. 1965. 'The Abolition of the Taboo System in Hawaii'. *Journal of the Polynesian Society* 74:21–39.

Williams, J. n.d.(a). 'Account of the Overthrow of Idolatry in the Island of Aitutaki, by Mr. John Williams, Missionary at Raiatea, Chiefly Taken Down from the Mouth of Papeiaha [*sic*], one of Two Native Teachers Left at Aitutaki in the Year 1821'. *Quarterly Chronicle* III:12–24 and 43–55.

———. n.d.(b). 'Translation of a Letter Received from Papeiha, Native Teacher at Rarotonga'. *Quarterly Chronicle* IV:291–93.

———. 1838. *A Narrative of Missionary Enterprises in the South Sea Islands: With Remarks Upon the Natural History of the Islands, Origin, Languages, Traditions, and Usages of the Inhabitants.* London: John Snow.

———. 1839. *Narrative of Missionary Enterprises in the South Seas: With Remarks Upon the Natural History of the Islands, Origin, Languages, Traditions and Usages of the Inhabitants.* London: John Snow.

Wilson, J. 1799. *A Missionary Voyage to the Southern Pacific Ocean Performed in the Years 1796, 1797, 1798, in the Ship Duff.* London: T. Chapman.

Index